VIRUS CITY

Published by Big Shoulders Books
DePaul University
Chicago, Illinois

ISBN: 979-8-218-02329-4
Library of Congress Control Number: 2022937682

Big Shoulders Books logo design by Robert Soltys

VIRUS CITY

CHICAGO 2020-2021

Edited by Rebecca Johns and Robin Hoecker   Foreword by Kenyatta Rogers

ABOUT BIG SHOULDERS BOOKS

Big Shoulders Books aims to produce one book each year that engages intimately with the Chicago community and, in the process, gives graduate students in DePaul University's Master of Arts in Writing and Publishing program hands-on, practical experience in book publishing. The goal of Big Shoulders Books is to disseminate, free of charge, quality anthologies of writing by and about Chicagoans whose voices might not otherwise be shared. Each year, Big Shoulders Books hopes to make small but meaningful contributions to discussions of injustice and inequality in Chicago, as well as to celebrate the tremendous resilience and creativity found in all areas of the city.

The views and opinions expressed in this book do not necessarily reflect those of DePaul University or the College of Liberal Arts and Social Sciences, and should not be considered an endorsement by DePaul for any purpose.

ABOUT OUR FUNDERS

Virus City: Chicago 2020–2021 was made possible by a grant from the William & Irene Beck Charitable Trust.

VIRUS CITY EDITORIAL STAFF

REBECCA JOHNS
EDITOR

ROBIN HOECKER
EDITOR

GILLIAN SCOTT
COPY EDITOR

NATALIE MILLS BONTUMASI
DESIGNER

ASSISTANT EDITORS
MEGAN ANDERSON
CAMRYN BEACO
ELVINA BESLAGIC
AMELIA BOWEN
DESIRAE BROOKS
JIMMY CHEN
CHELSEA COPELAND
MIRIAM CORTINOVIS
CAITLIN COSTELLO
MARIA DORADO
SAMUEL ECKERT
GARRETT EICHER
ZOË EITEL
ELLE EVANS
SARAH FINCK
ZOEY FINK
SAVANNAH GEER
ANNA GERWIG
JOHN GIESA
PAIGE GILBERG

ELIANA HERMAN
JESSICA KERN
ANNA KLINGMAN
ANNA KUBIK
MARINA KYRIAKOPOULOS
TORI LEVINE
CONNOR LINDSEY
LILY LOWNDES
JESSICA MACY
CHRISTY MARGESON
ALISON MATAYOSIAN
MARIA MAYNEZ
TONI MCELRATH
CHAZMEIR MIXON
DANIELLE MOORE
UKIAH MOOSES
WILLIAM NOEL
CHARLOTTE PEREZ
MALIK PITCHFORD
EMILY RICHARDS
RUBEN ROJAS
NOELLE ROSA
DAVID ROUBALIK
ELIZABETH RUDA
SARA SHAHEIN
JENNA SHATTUCK
TOM SHERIDAN
KAYLA SPENCER
TIMOTHY UNDERWOOD
JANELLE VASQUEZ
NICOLE VON DRASEK
MAREN WILBURN

Contents

INTRODUCTION REBECCA JOHNS..........ix

INTRODUCTION ROBIN HOECKER.........xii

FOREWORD KENYATTA ROGERS..........xiv

A PLEASURE TO SERVE EUGENIA SANDERS **1**

ZERO TO ONE HUNDRED "STEPHANIE" **9**

THEY'RE NOT CLIENTS, THEY'RE KIDS FRANK TEMPONE **15**

A BEACON OF HOPE HAROLD HAGERMAN **21**

PERPETUAL MOTION STEVEN **29**

THROWN TO THE SHARKS "SARAH GREENE" **35**

YOU NEED TO GIGGLE LAURA **41**

NOBODY CAN TAKE AWAY THAT VOICE ÓSCAR SÁNCHEZ **49**

WHEN MY EYES WERE OPENED CHI NEWSON **57**

THE BIG YEAR NELSON MORRIS **63**

WHO SAW THIS COMING? SHARON HOLLIVAY-WHEELER **71**

HOW WE WANT TO GROW MEGAN MORRISON **77**

PHOTOGRAPHIC ESSAYS **81**

    SELF-HEALING DURING THE PANDEMIC JANE ANDREWS **82**

    FINDING BEAUTY IN NEW PLACES AMY DO **86**

    DOCUMENTING UNCERTAINTY MARÍA MARTA GUZMÁN **92**

    STILL I RISE LA'INDIA COOPER **96**

    CRAMPED QUARTERS BROOKE SIEVERS **104**

    CITY ON FIRE JONATHAN AGUILAR **108**

A LOT OF COMMITMENT SHEILA MORRIS **113**

I THOUGHT ONLINE WAS GOING TO BE FUN "ELENA GARCÍA" **121**

SOMEBODY THAT LOOKS LIKE YOU LEMONE LAMPLEY **125**

HISTORY REPEATS ITSELF "MYRNA" **133**

LIMBS OF A WHOLE SALOUMEH BOZORGZADEH **137**

THE SILENT PANDEMIC MEGAN BENNETT **143**

A BLESSING AND A CURSE MIRZA BAIG **149**

DO YOU EVER GET TO BE TREATED LIKE A HUMAN? ESTHER CLARK **153**

A DAY OF REST COREY BROOKS **159**

A LITTLE BIT OF KINDNESS AARON SMITH **165**

DON'T WATCH THE NEWS CELSO SALAMANCA **171**

LOOKING FOR LIGHT NIKA VAUGHAN **175**

SITTING DUCKS JAMES SWANSEY **181**

THE LENS OF HISTORY JIM CONLEY **187**

IF I BUMPED INTO MY FRESHMEN ON THE STREET "GENEVIEVE" **193**

THE LONG HAUL MARINA DEL RIOS **199**

ABOUT THE EDITORS **208**

Introduction

REBECCA JOHNS

LIKE THE SUBJECTS IN THIS BOOK, I had entirely different plans before the COVID-19 pandemic began. In January 2020, when I first sat down with my colleagues at Big Shoulders Books, it was to discuss an anthology focused on incarcerated people and their families. The idea was to go into prisons during the summer and fall of 2020, run writing seminars with DePaul students and faculty as workshop leaders, and choose from the pieces produced in those courses a selection of essays, poems, and stories to turn into an anthology.

It was a subject I'd been interested in for a long time but hadn't yet been able to pursue. With the help of leaders from the DePaul University Inside Out program like Drs. Helen Damon-Moore and Christina Rivers, students in DePaul's writing and publishing program would create an anthology by and about incarcerated individuals. It was wholly in keeping with the social-justice mission of Big Shoulders Books. We were excited to begin.

The first meetings to try to make the project a reality would happen in spring. But by March 12, 2020, DePaul—and the prisons we hoped to visit—locked down.

∷∷∷
∷∷∷∷ ∙∙

COVID-19 was not sneaky. The first reports coming from abroad in late 2019 and early 2020 made it clear this virus was something new and potentially dangerous, and that it was being spread by human contact. But plagues were the stuff of the distant past, like the Spanish flu in 1918, or else the distant future. We were used to pandemics appearing in science fiction books and in the movies, but not real life. The idea that it could touch us was still, somehow, unthinkable.

As time went on, the prisons became a vector for spreading the virus. The Marshall Project, a nonprofit journalism institute dedicated to criminal justice reporting, estimated that by December 2020, one in five US prisoners had contracted COVID-19.[1]

.

---

[1] Source: https://www.themarshallproject.org/2020/12/18/1-in-5-prisoners-in-the-u-s-has-had-covid-19

Like many people, I kept hoping that a few weeks or even a couple of months of lockdown would be enough to flatten the curve and that life would return to normal in time to get the incarceration anthology going again. Even as protests broke out in spring 2020 over the death of George Floyd in Minneapolis, I kept in contact with the Inside Out team at DePaul and leadership at Restore Justice Illinois, a nonprofit group dedicated to criminal justice reform that had offered to contribute to the incarceration anthology project.

Though the situation in Chicago in general—not to mention inside the criminal-justice system—seemed to get more tense as protest after protest sprang up, I kept hoping that if we were able run workshops at Cook County Jail and Stateville Correctional Center and others, we'd probably still have enough time to produce the pieces we needed for the anthology. But as fall grew cold and the second COVID-19 wave began, we started to realize the prisons were not likely to let us inside anytime soon. Like everyone else, we had to pivot.

It was clear that the COVID-19 pandemic itself would become the topic for this anthology. How was this once-in-a-lifetime event affecting the everyday lives of Chicagoans? How did they cope with the physical, psychological, social, and economic tribulations brought on by COVID-19 in their jobs, in their families?

Throughout 2021, thirty-three DePaul students (graduate and undergraduate) recorded interviews with ordinary Chicagoans in a multitude of different professions and neighborhoods. Most of these interviews took place via Zoom, which—in addition to being the tool that kept us all attending classes—allowed students to meet their subjects while maintaining a safe social distance.

The students turned these Zoom recordings into transcripts, then into written narratives, thinking deeply and carefully about the words of each subject and, whenever possible, returning for a second interview. The final versions were edited by twenty-two graduate students in DePaul's Master's in Writing and Publishing program during the fall of 2021. We then forwarded the finished narratives to their respective subjects for a final fact check and review.

Our collective task was to honor the voice and intent of each speaker. On occasion, this includes leaving in profanity or non-standard English usage, a result of our decision not to censor our interviews. In a couple of instances, we did grant the subjects' requests for a pseudonym or used only a first name to protect their ability to speak honestly about their work without fear of retaliation from an employer or others.

Our working thesis for this project was that the pandemic was exacerbating the inequalities that already existed in our society, and these narratives show that those inequalities continue to affect the lives of many Chicagoans. The frustration and exhaustion of each speaker comes through in their voices. How much more can they take? When will anything go back to normal?

In the process of gathering these narratives, however, we also found unexpected joy.

Healthcare workers, retail workers, business owners, teachers, first responders, and former prison inmates: the people whose stories you will read in this anthology have been giving their all during the COVID-19 pandemic. They are parents to young children and caregivers to elderly parents. They have been treating patients and restocking shelves and warehouses. They have been teaching classes and holding religious services and putting out fires both literal and figurative. They have been feeding and clothing and treating and sheltering Chicago's residents in some of their most desperate hours.

It's a privilege to share their stories here.

I'd hoped by the time this volume appeared, we would have turned the final corner on COVID-19. The disease has been crossing the world in waves, first in spring 2020, then in autumn. Falling cases in the spring of 2021 and the first mass vaccinations gave us all hope that we were finally going to get back to normal, whatever that was likely to mean.

Then the Delta variant surged in the summer of 2021, Omicron around Christmas. In early 2022 the Omicron wave started to ease, with case positivity levels in Illinois beginning to decline.[2] Mask mandates were lifted in schools across the state.[3]

But COVID will likely be with us for a long time to come: on the day I sent *Virus City* to press—less than two weeks after the end of the Illinois school mask mandate—my own daughter, an eighth grader, tested positive for COVID. No longer the realm of science fiction, the pandemic has made us all exhausted and wary.

Someday life will go back to normal, though normal may not look like it did before. Perhaps it shouldn't. The pandemic has exposed the shaky foundations of our social order and maybe given us new insight into a way forward.

After all, a pivot—once made—takes you forever in a new direction.

[2] https://chicago.suntimes.com/coronavirus/2022/1/27/22905181/illinois-coronavirus-chicago-omicron-surge-cases-deaths-hospital-vaccine-arwady

[3] https://www.nbcchicago.com/news/coronavirus/are-masks-still-required-in-schools-what-to-know-about-cdc-guidance-illinois-mask-mandate/2769968/

Introduction

ROBIN HOECKER

WHEN THE PANDEMIC HIT IN MARCH OF 2020, I had no idea what was coming. As the city shut down, I quickly scrambled to shift my photojournalism classes online. To my surprise, the technology aspect of this process was the least challenging part. I had taught online before and already had some recorded lectures and assignments.

For me, the first challenge was the lack of child care. My daughter was just five at the time, in the middle of kindergarten at our neighborhood Chicago public school. Starting in March of 2020, my daughter and her classmates did not go to in-person school for a year and a half. We worked next to each other at the kitchen counter every day. She needed a lot of help with reading and remote learning. I worried that she was falling behind, or that I wasn't doing enough to help her. When I focused on her, I felt like I was failing at work.

As with many women during the pandemic, this situation took a toll.[4] I tried to balance being a professor, a mom, and my daughter's teacher and best friend all at the same time. I also had several friends and acquaintances pass away during this time, and was unable to properly grieve in community. My mental and physical health started to deteriorate. Even today, I am still recovering.

The second challenge was lockdown. How could I teach students photojournalism when they couldn't leave their apartments? In photojournalism, the general rule is, "If your pictures aren't good enough, you're not close enough."[5] But in a pandemic, being in close proximity suddenly became risky for both photographers and their subjects. I experimented with virtual portraiture, where photographers work with their subjects through video chats to set up portraits using smartphones.[6] Out

---

[4] Many studies and articles have been published showing how the pandemic has disproportionately affected women. Source: https://www.forbes.com/sites/tracybrower/2021/04/18/women-and-the-pandemic-serious-damage-to-work-health-and-home-demands-response/?sh=640bb7031f49
[5] This phrase was made famous by the legendary war photographer, Robert Capa. Source: https://pro.magnumphotos.com/C.aspx?VP3=CMS3&VF=MAGO31_9_VForm&ERID=24KL535353
[6] I wrote about teaching remote portraiture during the pandemic for an academic journal, *Teaching Journalism & Mass Communication*. Source: https://www.proquest.com/docview/2569699284

of necessity, I relaxed my ethics rules and let students photograph themselves, their roommates, and their families for assignments—something I had never allowed before.

Suddenly, I had a window into students' lives like I had never seen. With students spread out across the city, the country, and even the world, it was obvious that their situations were drastically different. Inequities that I knew about in theory appeared before my eyes. To be clear, I don't think the pandemic has been easy for anyone, but it had a disproportionate impact on people and communities that were already marginalized. Some students and their families worked on the front lines of the pandemic. Others lost their jobs and had major financial concerns. Some took on child-care duties for relatives while schools and day cares were closed. Others struggled with isolation or lack of internet access. Race and racism, and the demonstrations against police brutality after George Floyd's death in May 2020, exacerbated all of these tensions.

Alongside hardship, I also saw joy, strength, and resilience. Students reflected that they were re-evaluating what was important in their lives. They found beauty in small things. They came to terms with what they could control and what they could not. They found strength within themselves.

I wish more people could see what I am seeing, I thought as I reviewed their assignments.

That summer, I asked my students if they would be interested in sharing some of their work. I ended up publishing a visual essay using their photos with their permission.[7] I received a lot of encouraging feedback about how meaningful it was to document this time in history. Students' work from this period will also be archived with DePaul University's library collection about the pandemic.

When I learned of the *Virus City* project, I thought it would be the perfect place to share some more of these stories in-depth. I selected these stories based on a number of factors. First was the quality of their work. These students did a remarkable job documenting their lives, some equipped with just camera phones.

Second, these stories reflect some of the diversity of experiences of DePaul students at the time. These students lived in different neighborhoods and faced many challenges, but they met those challenges with incredible resilience.

Ultimately, I drew strength and inspiration from their stories, and I hope that you do too.

---

[7] I published this photo essay on Poynter, a journalism education website. https://www.poynter.org/reporting-editing/2020/student-reflections-photographs-coronavirus-protests/

Foreword

KENYATTA ROGERS

We all—all of us, every one of us—have stories. During the pandemic, we've all been looking for a silver lining. There have been a lot of positive things to come from COVID-19: student loans have been deferred several times, and it's a renter's market, with landlords more open to negotiating with tenants. There have also been a variety of stimulus checks; a couple of mine paid for all of my moving expenses, as I did one of the most adult things I have ever done in my life and hired movers.

But with all that, there has been a lot of hurt, a lot of trauma and a lot of uneasiness left over from COVID-19, and it will take a while for us to get over it. A lot of us have learned it's OK to not be OK. It's OK to cry, and OK to talk to someone. It's OK to feel lonely, and to grieve our lives. And it's OK to be selfish, to want to take care of ourselves, even if that means eating a whole tray of fudge brownies in bed or subscribing to streaming services and binge-watching whatever comes across the "recommended for you" category.

For me, my ups and my downs start with what I can't see and what I can. It feels like the whole world collapsed and I'm stuck under a mile-high stack of rubble. I can't imagine being in a crowded bar, let alone ever again walking into one with all of my friends.

I have friends who have been vaccinated and some who haven't. I have friends who are vaccinated and have relatives who aren't. I have friends who are vaccinated but still are afraid of all the unknowns. In winter, going outside means leaving the house to go inside some other place. I have friends who are unvaccinated and can't go outside. I can only speak for myself, but I doubt many people would disagree that the past two years have been hard. The past two years have calcified all the things that life was and feels like life will ever be again.

A friend of mine said, "We might as well buckle up and sit back, because this is how it's going to be." And that's scary, and also so real right now. Everything we are experiencing is becoming normalized. Whenever I go to my job, or to get my locs retwisted, or to the spa, to movies and restaurants, I literally and metaphorically get a gun pointed at my head. It's normal procedure now for me to be triggered on a daily basis. To say things have been hard might not be enough. For anyone to try to put words together to make sense of anything in the past two years seems entirely impossible.

The definition of inconceivable is "not capable of being imagined or grasped mentally." A few years ago, COVID-19 would have seemed like something out of a science fiction novel. And for some, trying to grasp the now is still inconceivable. We are all suffering, and I can only imagine we will have some sort of mass trauma to overcome for many years to come.

I have a friend whom I work with who eats lunch in a room by himself with the windows open in the dead of winter. His grandmother got COVID-19 twice, and his uncle was in the hospital on a respirator. He says it's not like he doesn't want to hang out or get together, just that he has had too many people who are susceptible, and he needs to be very cautious.

I told him that's always going to be the case, that they are always going to be at risk, and he's always going to have to take care of himself. No matter what, COVID-19 is not going away. It's beyond woven into the fabric—it's stitched into our skins.

I'm a schoolteacher and am around hundreds of people on a daily basis. It's like being a matador who can't see the bull: not blind, but not able to see the danger, yet knowing it's there. I'm put in the face of death every day. And I know I'm not the only one. I see my students and know their stories are all individual, unique, and different.

I have a student who lives with five other people who (except for her) all caught COVID-19 at the same time. I have a friend who has to quarantine almost every couple of weeks because of close contact. I've also known a lot of people who quit their jobs and live parts of their bucket list that they never would have gotten the chance to do before: rock climbing in Colorado, or decking out a van to live in. They can be anyplace at any given time, and when it's time to duck out, go.

What I'm trying to say is, I have a unique story and experiences, but so do a lot of other people. They are stories that people were unprepared to live, let alone tell. This collection is full of people who are telling their stories with honesty and in earnest. You'll be reading about firefighters and EMTs who see death and pain on a daily basis and have to be around groups of people; a worker at an adolescent psychiatric inpatient facility who watches his students find some other home to go to; teachers and students who were thrown into online learning with little to no preparation, and how that has created worry about an uncertain future; or a student working in Chinatown who now has to deal not only with the stress of work, but also with prejudice and hate against Asian-Americans.

This collection is about human beings living and struggling, but most importantly, overcoming. This collection is about more than the human condition. It's about human resiliency.

Sanders sat for a Zoom interview with the sound of kids playing on skateboards wafting in through an open window. Soft-spoken and warm, Sanders was quick with a laugh and a smile.

A Pleasure to Serve

EUGENIA SANDERS, MD, PEDIATRICIAN

When Chicago Mayor Lori Lightfoot announced at the beginning of the COVID-19 pandemic that homeless Chicagoans needing to practice social distancing would be housed in several empty downtown hotels[8], Eugenia Sanders, MD, decided she would volunteer to treat their medical issues. Sanders, a pediatrician with the Lawndale Christian Health Center and a longtime member of the Apostolic Faith Church in Bronzeville[9] and its medical ministry group, had suddenly found herself with few patients but a huge need to feel useful.

More than a year later, on the first warm spring day of 2021, Sanders sat for a Zoom interview with the sound of kids playing on skateboards wafting in through an open window. Soft-spoken and warm, Sanders was quick with a laugh and a smile.

I'M ONE OF THE SITE MEDICAL DIRECTORS for the pediatric team for Lawndale.[10] We kept hearing different things and kept thinking, "Uh oh. What's going on in Europe?" and other countries that were dealing with lockdowns. Of course, December [2019] we heard about the first cases in China, so we were learning about COVID-19 and what that meant. Just being a medical health professional, I knew about it to some degree but wasn't really taking it too seriously.

One of my friends from college has a family member who is over in Europe, and she was like, "They're on lockdown." [She] told [me] we'd be there in a couple of weeks. I was kind of skeptical.

It hit all of a sudden one day. We had our medical director meeting, and they were like, "We've got to figure out how we're going to deal with this." We have an annual meeting. We were going to have it in our senior center, so they were like, "We can't do it there." Because seniors

[8] Source: https://chicago.cbslocal.com/2020/03/23/5-chicago-hotels-to-house-the-homeless-with-covid-19/

[9] Bronzeville on Chicago's South Side was an early-twentieth century cultural hub for the city's Black population. Among its many famous residents are musician Louis Armstrong, aviation pioneer Bessie Coleman, author Richard Wright, poet Gwendolyn Brooks, and activist Ida B. Wells. Source: https://interactive.wttw.com/dusable-to-obama/bronzeville

[10] Lawndale Christian Health Center serves the Lawndale community on Chicago's West Side. Source: https://lawndale.org/

are there. We were just trying to figure out what's the strategy to move forward with seeing patients.

I think one of the directors, his son had got sent home from college. Everybody was seeing it was getting more serious, of course, and then the NBA game [got] canceled.[11] Everything was happening.

We broke up into different teams to have meetings to teach our support staff— trying to allay their fears and having individual separate meetings, versus one big meeting—to try to answer questions and explain what the coronavirus was.

That was kind of the first [meeting] of many. I think the debate about the masks was on that table too. Some people were like, "You need to wear a mask." Some were like, "You don't." Just a whole bunch of that.

········
·········· ··
·········

The week before, I went to the movies with one of my friends. Then right when things really hit, I got sick, so then I was like, *OK, I shouldn't have gone to the movies.* I couldn't really be a part of the further planning as far as the shutdowns. They started canceling appointments and canceling in-person visits and trying to move to more telemedicine, so I was just home, hanging out, waiting.

[I didn't have COVID then], I just had cold symptoms. I got sick right at the time when they want you to stay home if you have any symptoms. Things were just crazy.

I was out for seven days. Then by the time I came back, it was like a ghost town.

We learned about how to do telemedicine. [We got] training on that, but I didn't really like the telemedicine at first because, for pediatrics, it was just hard to schedule patients. [Parents] were just busy, maybe focusing on their school. We weren't really getting a lot of reasons to see patients for telehealth.

Today, we have plenty of patients for telemedicine, but when it first started, it was really hard to fill our schedules. At that time, of course, [pediatrics] wasn't really a big risk factor as far as kids getting COVID and getting severe symptoms and dying. The need for us was like, "Well, you guys don't have a lot to do." We were just seeing newborns and less-than-a-year visits in-person. Our job was like, "What should we do?" We were on the sidelines.

Like I said, I didn't really like the telemedicine because we didn't have a lot of patients that were scheduled, and [my supervisors] were complaining because we were just sitting at home doing nothing, which was fine with me. But they didn't like us being at home and not seeing patients. We were supposed to try to contact

---

11 The NBA suspended the remainder of the 2019-2020 season on March 11, 2020, after several players tested positive for COVID-19. Source: https://www.nba.com/news/coronavirus-pandemic-causes-nba-suspend-season

and put them in [the schedule], but I didn't really enjoy that. I don't really feel like going to people and trying to get them to get on the phone for a visit, you know?

Then [I was] trying to get used to being at home because I've always been very busy, both at church and at work. I was kind of like, Oh, nothing to do. It was a little bit of an adjustment.

Then at the same time, our clinic partnered with the city to serve the homeless in a hotel. I've always wanted to help and be useful. I sent an email to one of the directors, like, "If you guys need help, I want to help, do what I can." Then maybe about a week later, my director gave me a phone call. They were like, "We're not sure there's going to be any kids there," but I was like, "OK, well, if there's a need."

I think they had a huge influx of homeless people in the hotel, maybe two hundred, and they had gotten some of the other providers who see adults to be a part of that project. They needed more help, so they were like, "Maybe we ask the pediatricians, a couple of them, to join the hotel team."

I was one of the first pediatric providers to join. It ended up being three of us: me, another pediatrician, and a pediatric nurse practitioner. [We were] basically just seeing adults from then on—homeless men and women, no children—from April to September [2020].

The program was great. The city helped us to get housing for many of the people who were homeless, and they went to different shelters and had some come stay at the hotel[12] to keep them safe whenever there were outbreaks [in] different places, like the Salvation Army or Pacific Garden Mission.[13] Several different homeless shelter [populations] came there, were invited to come stay at the hotel for safety. So we rounded[14] with them every day to see that they were getting what they needed. We brought them their food because they had to stay in their hotels. When the [COVID-19] cases were high, we had to bring them everything or go do their errands. They'd want us to go pick up something that they might need.

It was a great experience. I got to do adult medicine for a change, get back into that. I was grateful for that, and I was grateful to get out of the house, even though some people were like, "Well, that's pretty scary," because, I mean, some of those patients may have had COVID.

We saw some people that had some diagnoses that had been on the back burner, that we couldn't catch in time, so that was sad. Diabetes, high blood pressure, cancer.

[12] Sanders saw patients at the Hotel 166 on E. Superior St. in Chicago during the time it was used as a homeless shelter. Source: https://www.chicagotribune.com/news/breaking/ct-hotels-166-chicago-homeless-20200511-q3rxmmzarvbwbdkprhxjhsfwjm-story.html

[13] Pacific Garden Mission on the South Side operates several homeless shelters and ministry programs to aid the homeless population of Chicago. Source: https://www.pgm.org/

[14] Rounds involves a daily meeting with the patient and their medical team to keep up to date on care.

We would go knock on their doors every morning and check in, make sure that their vitals were stable and make sure that they were doing OK. We had a lot of mental health challenges. One patient was having a lot of delusions. We've had to have the police come to assist.

It was a scary time for everyone in the beginning with the concerns over getting COVID. The homeless guests appreciated having their own room with their television and all that, even though there were restrictions. They couldn't go outside the hotel as much as they would have liked.

They were able to go out more as the numbers went down, got to go out on day passes. We implemented our fitness staff to work with the guests by providing exercise as our clinic fitness center was closed due to the pandemic. The staff came and worked with them, and we had times when they would go to the rooftop deck and be able to exercise. There were pizza parties and talent shows as well, as a way to make it pleasant for them.

Sometimes, you knock on the door [to hear], "My stomach hurts," "I have a rash," "My foot needs this," so we were able to have additional services such as podiatry and behavioral health services available to assist with evaluations when needed.

We were supposed to, initially, just be [seeing patients] who weren't really having major medical problems. Over time, it kind of morphed into a variety of different illnesses. The experience definitely revealed some of the disparities within the homeless population and the need for adequate health care at all times.

That was most of my COVID experience. It was rewarding. We provided food, clothing, books, activities, lots of different things to keep the guests interested or keep them engaged. We did our best to try to provide a great experience for them and shelter them from COVID disease.

I was sad to see the program end. It is one of my most memorable or treasured experiences. I really enjoyed serving the homeless population and being a part of the team. We had a wonderful time.

In July, we started going back maybe once a week. I did [telehealth] when I was still at the hotel because you could do that any time. I tried to keep up with a few patients. September, once the hotel project ended, I went back to my regular [schedule], but it's still only twice a week at most that I'm in the clinic.

For our pediatric team, we have maybe ten or eleven providers. Everybody can't be there at the same time. Especially when the cases increased in the winter season, November [2020], we limited the number of providers so we don't have too many patients overcrowding the waiting area.

I've had about five patients who ended up with MIS-C,[15] which is the multi-inflammatory syndrome, so the more severe COVID symptoms. I've had some that have just had COVID, but then I've had some with the MIS-C, where they had to be admitted. They've had a whole bunch of inflammatory reactions, fever, stomach pain. One I thought sounded like appendicitis and I was like, "Oh, you need to go to the hospital." Ultimately, it ended up being COVID, multi-inflammatory syndrome. Thankfully, though, they've all recovered. My youngest was two years old, who had to be admitted to the ICU.[16]

After I got back to my regular work, I worked at times at the testing site, so I'll do COVID testing, drive-through testing. I would do that sometimes or do telemedicine. Now that we have the vaccine, I do give out the vaccine about once a week.

With African Americans, there has been hesitancy [about getting vaccinated]. For our church population, because our pastor is a physician[17] and a trusted leader and very knowledgeable about COVID, he's been educating the church through Zoom calls about COVID from the beginning. He has worked tirelessly to help people to overcome their fears about research, try to educate them about Tuskegee[18] and the difference from then versus now. He's been doing a lot to prepare people so that when the vaccine came—for those that truly listened to him—I don't know that there was a lot of hesitancy among most of them. I won't say 100 percent, [because] I do know people that still are like, "I'm healthy. I don't have to get it." You know, there are just people that are set in their ways, or they just have their beliefs about vaccines or about the government.

We face that a lot because we give out flu vaccines every year, so we can often get a lot of pushback about vaccinations. Our pastor makes the announcement like, "It doesn't give you the flu." He gives a spiel about that, but then we still get people that are walking past, "Nope. Don't want it. I never got it. I've never had the flu."

---

[15] There are two types of multisystem inflammatory syndrome caused by COVID-19: MIS-A (for adults), and MIS-C (for children). It is a rare but serious condition associated with COVID-19 in which different body parts become inflamed, including the heart, lungs, kidneys, brain, skin, eyes, or gastrointestinal organs. Source: https://www.cdc.gov/mis/index.html

[16] Intensive Care Unit

[17] Bishop Horace Smith, MD, pastor of the Apostolic Faith Church in Bronzeville, is an attending physician specializing in pediatric hematology/oncology at Ann & Robert H. Lurie Children's Hospital of Chicago. Source: https://www.afcchicago.org/drhoracesmith

[18] The US Public Health Service Syphilis Study at Tuskegee began in 1932 and involved six hundred Black men—399 of whom had syphilis and 201 who did not—without their informed consent. When penicillin became a widely available treatment for syphilis in the 1940s, the Tuskegee participants were not offered any treatment. Source: https://www.cdc.gov/tuskegee/timeline.htm

I think it's just helpful as well [that] we have our pastor, who is a doctor. It starts from him, so then we can just come in there and reinforce what he's told us or what he's told the congregation so that it helps people to be more trusting, like they're on the same page and they're in healthcare. People in our church know us.

We do what we can to try to keep educating, but I find that, in general...our coworkers still are like, "I'm just getting mine today." I'm like, "It's May. OK." You know? We had it since January, but you know.

We did a lot as well with our job. We had a lot of information sessions and lunchtime teaching just to try to help educate and not make people feel like you got to do it but just try to... I think you just have to do a lot of education about it, around it, so that people feel more comfortable.

There's a lot of people that, for whatever reasons, they're like, "Can't—too soon." You know? All these different [feelings] people have about it.

∷∷∷∷ ∷ ∷ •••
∷∷∷∷∷∷∷

I've been trying to work on saying no. When the virus hit, this gave me good reasons to say no, because I always tend to say yes to things, even to my detriment. I feel like if somebody invited me here or there, I've got to go. I guess I have trouble with boundaries. I was busy in church doing several different things. I teach Sunday school for the teenagers, and I work with our health ministry. I'm one of the ministers there. I'm also one of the group leaders for congregational life for our church.

That's the other thing as well—how we stay connected is through the congregational life,[19] which is a small group. We used to meet once a month. When COVID hit, we changed it to meet twice a month. That was more responsibility on us, but that's OK. It's not horrible, but it's a little something on top of the other things that I had.

When the virus did hit, I did have to say no. I stopped teaching Sunday school for a bit because it was too many transitions, trying to figure out how we were going to do that on Zoom. We had to change it to be a PowerPoint. Before we would just go in the class and you had to prepare, but you had the students in front of you reading through the book or talking. I couldn't manage all of that transition on top of everything else.

That allowed me some breathing room. Then with the health ministry, we did a weight-loss program that got switched to virtual. We kept that going with the presentations and finished that with the finale walk in July [2020] outdoors. That turned out well in spite of COVID.

---

[19] Small groups at Apostolic Faith Church that organize community-service projects. Source: https://www. afcchicago.org/clife

I guess, for me, I think I'm trying to learn that I have to find a balance. I don't want to go back to just doing everything to the point of not taking care of myself, because as I learned, I think when COVID first came, I was used to always going. You're so used to having something to do. Becoming a part of the hotel project just made sense. Of course, I just had a passion. I wanted to serve there and help.

Also, just not having all those responsibilities has been helpful....When people try to push more things back—"Let's get this back to doing this"—I'm like, "Oh, my goodness, let's ease into that." I don't want to get back to the degree of where I was. I'm still trying to figure out how that looks. I want to be where I am balanced, where I'm able to do things that I want to do—take care of my parents, check on them—and not feel like I got this obligation. I guess I'm just still trying to figure out how to keep a good balance with work and everything else.

[My parents] don't need me to take care of them per se. They're up in age. Sometimes I do have to take them to their doctors' appointment. I took my dad to get his COVID vaccine. He has arthritis and Parkinson's. He's had some hip pains, so I don't know if the doctors want him to, but he wants to get a hip replacement. I have to take him more than my mom. She likes to go on her own. She's kind of independent. She's 78 and he's 87.

My dad likes to get out of the house because they're retired, but he likes to go out and get his own stuff. Mother didn't have trouble learning how to use the grocery app, but my dad likes to get the groceries and get out. I'd be like, "Don't go." I had to fight with them to be like, "This is serious. You don't want to get COVID."

He's like, "I'm safe. I don't go anywhere. I just get the groceries and come back home." It's a whole thing that he just had to get out, whereas my mom is like, "I'm fine." She's not opening the door, not going anywhere. I guess because of the Parkinson's he needed to get out because he gets stiff. With arthritis too, he gets stiff. I guess he fell one time because he didn't get out. My mother was like, "Well, he just needs to get out so he can move around." I had to let that go and stop trying to keep them totally safe, but thank God, they have been fine. They didn't get COVID. They got their vaccine.

I've had a couple of losses of people that passed away from COVID. One was a close family member. That was just devastating and sad.

That always makes me pause when people are like, "I don't know if I want the vaccine." I'm like, "Don't you realize all the lives that are lost in this time?" [It's] nothing to play with. I wish people would take it seriously, or watch the news and see all of the families who experienced their losses.

Looking back on it, I appreciate the opportunity to serve and to be a part of the team that was able to serve those patients. I'm grateful for those that were able to get housing, get back on their feet, and get support services. We had one person that was deaf. I enjoyed connecting with him, as we can, through the interpreters.

It was our pleasure to serve them every day and just let them know that they're not by themselves as they're in this housing place, trying to keep from getting COVID. It was a rewarding experience to care for them and to see them through.

—REBECCA JOHNS

Zero to One Hundred

"STEPHANIE," FIREFIGHTER & EMT

Stephanie (not her real name) has been a firefighter and EMT for eleven years and has spent the time learning to remain as stress-free as possible.

When I talked with her at the beginning of 2021, Stephanie explained how the struggles of 2020 impacted her already-hectic life as a mother and firefighter.

GIRL, COVID JUST PALES IN COMPARISON TO ME. I never stopped going to work. I didn't quarantine because we couldn't. There's no such thing as firemen and policemen not coming to work. I hear "essential worker" and I'm thinking, *Yeah, we're doing our job.* It never changed.

I speak for myself, but it was just another thing we had to deal with. It's almost damn near impossible for us not to get [COVID], because if nine COVID patients call us, we're going to nine COVID patients' houses. You can take the measures, but it just is what it is. Girl, no mask will prevent COVID like that.

We all laugh about it, because we just feel like we do our job every time, no matter what's out there. We laugh about this type of stuff because we understand the severity of the work we do. You could cry about it, you could moan, but you just need find a space where you could find joy. And hope the next call is not the last call.

Work is work. We don't get to say, "I'm not going to do that, or I'm not coming to work because I'm sick, or tired." We don't have that luxury. For me, only thing changed was now we need to be a little cleaner, which we needed to be anyway. We've already lost so many, you know? We've lost brothers and sisters on this job, that's so real and eye opening.

Firemen have this ridiculous view on life. Sometimes it hurts us and sometimes it helps us, but we don't really think about ourselves. We just think about other people.

So, we started wearing the masks more, because you don't want to take it home. So, [with] COVID it wasn't a huge adjustment other than just being compliant. Wear our masks, wash our hands, make sure we take certain precautions.

You've got to remember we go from zero to one hundred. We run into burning buildings. The things that people never see, we've seen. The things that people never experience. Death on such a great scale. Especially seeing so many young Black men getting killed.

I had to go seek counseling in my third year. The amount of death that we see on a daily basis is not normal for anybody, and the pressures of being a mother, not having an outlet for what was going on at work—it started to take a toll on my life, so I had to go see a professional. I'm an advocate for it because it saved my life.

For work, I get up in the morning at five so I can be there at six. Relief of the next guy is at seven, then roll call is at eight. You want to get your gear in service, hook up your mask, and make sure your tank is working, because that's your lifeline. You never want to play with that. And then we go have coffee, and it's time for us to start the day. Once you put yourself in service, anything can happen for your twenty-four hours. No matter what, we make those calls.

It's super intense because you're new, you don't know much, and you don't want to make a mistake. But you have a family. Every workday for the last eleven years, I've pretty much had the same guys except for the guys that got promoted or transferred out the house. Even though things are intense, you still have somebody you can depend on.

I don't want to sound cliché-ish, but my life kind of prepared me for this. My upbringing in my life prepared me. I had to go to church because my lights were off. I was about to get evicted; I didn't have a job. My baby daddy was horrible. I decided to go to church for the very first time at the New Year's Eve Service. I knew I couldn't be nowhere else because I didn't have nothing else.

When I decided to go to the service, I just prayed: Lord, could He please give me a job that could take care of my kids, so I don't have to ask nobody for nothing? Seven days later in the mail came a letter from the fire department. Like I said, my life was in shambles. And when my mother called me like, "You got a letter from the department. They asked you do you want a job?" It was all she wrote from that moment.

[I still had] obstacles to get there. The academy...it's parallel military. It was majority white men. All I can remember was [thinking], *They not getting this job back, baby. They are paying me fifty-five thousand dollars a year to walk through the door. I don't know what I'm doing. I ain't got a clue. I ain't never seen none of this in my life. But baby, y'all not gone take this from me.*

As much as we are together, we are divided sometimes. I navigated [politics] based on, *I don't care, I don't want to hear this*. We try not to bombard the firehouse with religion and politics, but sometimes it's unavoidable. You just must stick up for yourself. If you don't stand for something, you'll fall for anything.

You don't have to engage in every conversation, don't have to fight every battle. But some of them you do. Some things you do have to stand up for. Some things you do have to say, "That's not right." But when the bell rings, all bets are off. You're family. When the bell rings, I don't care if you Black, white, or pinstripe, everybody comes home.

I've never felt like my life was in danger at an incident because somebody wasn't protecting me. I got one of the houses where they care about me. Everything they taught me, I adopted it and gave it to somebody else. But they didn't play about me learning what I had to learn. For one, they didn't want me to have them looking bad. They didn't care who I was. Those are some of the best men I've ever met in my life. I've met some of the best men (next to my father) on this job. And I've met some of the worst ones too. It's two-sided.

But it's like anything else. If I went to work thinking everybody was against me, everybody would have probably been against me. But I didn't go to work like that because I don't take anything personally. Your problem with me is not my problem. Whatever you feel about me, you should probably deal with it with yourself because I don't really care. That's my approach to every day. For the most part, you make it work even with the racism, with the sexism, even with the ageism. You deal with it and then you go about your day.

I thank God every day, and I still have to pinch myself like, "Oh! I fight fires!" I get goosebumps. God, I'm at one of the best jobs in the world. And not because I get to see people at their worst or see destruction. It's because females look at me like, "Damn, I could do that." And I say, "You absolutely can." That's humbling to me. It's much bigger than me.

It's still a blessing to get off the rig and see little girls that look like you, and they are staring and you waving. I'm so big on representation. I follow the words "Being what I want to see," so if I want to see more people helping us, then I got to start with myself.

I think that work has probably prepared me more for my personal life. Because I'm not hysterical when I see certain things, blood or gunshots. You have that small area of homes, where you have very nice homes. Go two blocks over, you can hear gun shots at any moment. It's such a hodgepodge of people. And then you add COVID on top of that.

Your biggest concern is not to take [COVID] home to your family. My main goal was just making sure my kids stayed mentally healthy through this. But other than that, COVID didn't really do nothing but add. It didn't make us look at nothing different, just made us work harder. It never stopped for me; life never stopped. Having to deal with your personal stuff on top of work, the personal stuff supersedes.

My mother did get sick, but luckily, she made it through. She had double pneumonia in both her lungs, and then she had COVID as well. It was very scary. To have my mother in the hospital was one of those things where— That's the unknown to me, if something happens to my mother. She's my support system. Her and my dad been together for years, like they're still together. So, we are a close family.

That's the time where I display my emotions, when it's something going on with my children or my parents. I think that's when you see me shake, you know what I'm saying? That's when you can see me being vulnerable. At work you don't have the luxury.

∙∙∙∙∙∙∙
∙∙∙∙∙∙∙∙∙∙∙∙
∙∙∙∙∙∙∙∙∙

I worked during the protests.[20] They did tear up some stuff. It was probably the hardest day of my career simply because everything was on fire. So much was on fire. We didn't have the resources to take care of it. Trucks don't have water, but they were the only available bodies that we could send. [There] wasn't nothing they could really do but just look at [the fires]. That day tested my will and my strength, but I wouldn't have missed it. I would have still been there so I can still protect the people, still take care of people. If nothing else, when you pull up, you get to make sure it's OK.

You know it takes a brave person to get out there and do what we do. Like get out there and put yourself out there on the front lines. I'll run into a burning building first. I didn't know anybody that got out there [to] protest. But I'm glad I was on this side of it to help pick up the pieces, help mitigate and put out the fires. If that was my contribution, then I'll take that.

I'm just glad I was there to put them out. I don't think [there's] anything wrong with going out there and letting people know that you support a cause that's real, that affects you on a daily basis. But as far as the destruction of property, I don't agree with it.

---

[20] After bystanders videotaped Minneapolis police officer Derek Chauvin kneeling on the neck of George Floyd until he lost consciousness and died, protests against police brutality broke out across the United States. In Chicago, protests began on May 29, 2020 and lasted until June 7, 2020. Source: https://www.chicagotribune.com/news/breaking/ct-viz-george-floyd-protest-chicago-timeline-20200531-lfk-d7p6ejbennfezhxk2u5kkmm-story.html Source: https://www.chicagotribune.com/news/breaking/ct-george-floyd-chicago-protests-20200606-ee4mdvafvbfhfcpr7lrzfayypu-story.html

Any of the rioting, the protesting, any of the people's reasons, you got to look at the backlash of it with COVID added. And the most hurt are the elderly people that call us on a daily basis to pick them up off the floor, or take them up the stairs to their apartments, help them when they're sick.

That, to me, is the hardest part. They still need certain things, and they don't have it now. Thank you for opening the pharmacy back up, but I don't want to see our elderly men and women having to struggle to go get medicine. But that's the flip side of them doing what [the protesters] did. That's what people are not seeing right now. They're not seeing the aftereffects of what's happening in these communities. There were already food deserts. There's [people] hungry and starving.

So how do I complain about COVID? How do I complain about my issues that I can actually go fix, that I have the means to go fix? How do I complain when I go to work tomorrow to a senior citizen building, and I go into an apartment where somebody hasn't eaten in days? Like how do I complain? Everything else to me pales in comparison when it comes to what you really see, what you really go through. That's a real issue of COVID. Not me getting up, going to work, having to put this mask on every day. That's nothing. I get paid for my job. I took an oath to do my job. But you want to talk about an issue with COVID, let's talk about the communities. Let's talk about the [fact that the] people really affected are the young and old. That's the real issue to me.

— MAREN WILBURN

VIRUS CITY

Frank Tempone was sitting in his
home office, the lights behind him dim.
At 50, he has found his calling helping youth.
He has three children, who he says
have taught him to be a more compassionate
and effective teacher.

They're Not Clients, They're Kids

FRANK TEMPONE, ACADEMIC COORDINATOR

Frank Tempone was sitting in his home office, the lights behind him dim. At 50, he has found his calling helping youth. He has three children, who he says have taught him to be a more compassionate and effective teacher.

When we talked, he had just come home from an extended day at work in order to help a student in need. Tempone works at an adolescent psychiatric inpatient facility in the suburbs of Chicago that he prefers not to refer to by name. His experience working in a mental health facility has only been during the COVID-19 pandemic.

I WORK AT [AN INPATIENT FACILITY]. It's just overall services. While [the clients] are here, they have one-on-one and group therapy. They're fed well by a private chef who gives them three meals a day plus two snack-type meals. They have school with me, 8:30 a.m. to 12:30 p.m., every day. They're grouped [into tiers] and they do exercise, mostly off television. Other than that, they're in treatment and recovery.

Pre-COVID, I worked at the Latin School of Chicago for eleven years. In August [2020], I finished the [school] year and went to [the inpatient facility] to do something more meaningful with my life. At first, I didn't know how to write reports. So, I looked at some of my colleagues'. They always called the kids clients: the client, the client, the client. When we talk about them informally, my supervisor would say "the children." It was weird that way. I automatically call them students, but they're not students. They're not there to learn—they're there to recover.

My official title is academic coordinator. What that entails is when a student—when a client—comes in, my job is to keep them working on their academics, so they don't have to suffer more anxiety when they leave and are behind in all their classes. On top of the issues that they're having, the kids are constantly thinking, "Am I going to graduate?" "Am I going to pass ninth grade? Tenth grade?" So my job is to communicate with their schools and teach them things they need help with, but also help them maintain structure.

It's a money game for the [inpatient facility]. They want to [bring] kids in because insurance pays a lot of money per night. Being someone brand new with fresh eyes, that's what I'm seeing.

Once in a while, you'll hear, "This is going to be a good kid for this group." But a lot of the time, if these kids need a place to go and we have beds, then [inpatient facility] is just going to let them in and see what happens.

It surprised me that we closed for a month for COVID—[I was] shocked that they didn't try to open up and populate the place right away. Well, once we did open, they had six kids in a snap. I think we just discharged one kid today, and we're discharging a young woman tomorrow. I'm suspecting next week we'll have two or three more just to keep the business rolling.

[The kids] can't leave unless someone comes and picks them up. Their parents come, or they're taken away by the police or in an ambulance. And that's happened many times.

Or they run away. We had a kid just go, and we didn't know where he was. He's like, "I've had it!" and he left. The cops were all over the streets looking for him. He almost made it to his house. He went over the wall and took off. He escaped. And I don't know how he's doing now, but [the facility] didn't let him come back. He was a good boy too.

Kids tend to stay for about six or seven weeks. We have a tier system; it's a way for them to see that they are making progress in their treatment. The tiers go up to tier five, and we have tier meetings once a week. A client has to be there a full week and meet specific personal objectives before tiering up the first time. It's all staggered. It's good to have people at different tiers because they can help the others along.

We have someone who is at the top tier. She was just wonderful and is leaving tomorrow. She has been able to lead a couple of groups; that's one of the benefits of reaching tier five. We had some tier ones and tier twos. The kids can see that that's the end of the tunnel. They think, *I could get there. I could be happy, confident, and ready to go.* Now, it could all fall apart for her once she leaves if she doesn't have a stable system at home. But supposedly we have taken care of that.

The youngest we've gotten is 12, so sixth grade, and the oldest we've gotten is 17, so that's an issue. Sometimes you get a 12 and a 17, and they are in way different places, mainly brain development, their lives and interests. So that could be a little bit of an issue, especially if you have three or four 17-year-olds and one 12-year-old. That could be very lonely. And the other way around, one 17-year-old and a bunch of 12 and 13-year-olds, it can get lonely.

We were shut down in early November [2020]. I wasn't feeling well, and I had to actually call in sick. Before I could come back, I had to be tested. So, I went to DuPage County [for a COVID test]. It ended up coming back positive. I went back to the facility just to get my stuff, but someone came running out saying, "We're shutting down because all the kids ended up contracting it." I don't know how the heck that happened. Kids were just discharged to their parents, some being there for only two weeks. None of them had really bad symptoms, they just went home. It didn't really help them; it just threw them into instability.

But it shut us down for the month of November. We went back after Thanksgiving. We walk around with masks constantly. It seems to be going all right. Everyone gets their temperatures taken, and we record it every day. And those kids—they didn't come back. I don't think the company said, "We're not taking these kids back." I think [the parents] were like, "Forget it. I'm not sending my kid back there. No."

We got all new kids. They're not worried about [COVID]; their anxieties are taken up by other things. I think that a lot of other students are feeling the same way. They've heard that COVID is not affecting kids at the same rate, that kids don't get sick as much as adults. They want to get out. By the time they leave us, if they've gone through the program, they feel like they're ready to go and that mental health mountain was enough for them. They're not worried about COVID if they have gotten through that.

I had one client whose classmate, in a different grade, died of it. It was a pretty big story in the suburbs of Chicago. So that's always kind of disturbing.

[The kids] feel a lot of school-related stress when they first arrive, because usually they don't do any kind of school work when they're hospitalized. They're usually behind when they come to us. So when I get an email that says, "We're welcoming a new intake today," I immediately start working. I look for the school's consent paperwork and call the academic coordinator, saying, "This person is coming to me today. I'd like to collaborate with you. Here's the consent to exchange confidential information form. I want to hit the ground running."

I would imagine that it's a lot easier for the academic coordinator now. [Pre-COVID,] it must have been difficult working in this position, because everything had to be photocopied and sent by the school. There wasn't a ready-made online curriculum for the kids.

VIRUS CITY

But now, with Google Classroom, it's easy. Everybody does the same thing. I just have to say, "I think you should work on these three assignments today." As long as a student is enrolled, it's just a matter of getting their passwords, setting them up with headphones and a laptop, and making sure they're not going on TikTok.

In a way, the whole school being out has benefited them. They can appear on screen just like everyone else. Not to say that they're getting the same experience as students who go to school regularly and are in a classroom; that's the best way to learn. But if you're in therapy and your classmates know you're not there...

The situation that exists now is a little more palatable because they have their work there, they can do it. They don't get alternative assignments. Sometimes if they want to, they can join their classes. And it's not like: "Where's Lily? Lily's gone?" It's more like: "There's Lily. She's on the screen." I usually put them in a space where there's nothing in the background but the painted wall. So it's no one's business where they are.

But everything is online now—family therapy is online now. The only time we actually see the parents is at drop-off. And sometimes they're dropped off or picked up by an ambulance or the police. That's been the issue with screens. These kids come in to us, and they are going through the therapy. After a week or two, they buy into it and they're really trying to better themselves. But their parents, who also need to be in therapy along with them, have no problem with walking away when they don't want to be a part of things. You know, if Mom and Dad are on the screen and Dad's had enough, he will get up and leave.

I'm not a part of the therapeutic part of their day. The only firsthand experience I have of these meetings is reading the reports. It's important for me. I'm there and I'm always talking to them, but I'm not licensed. However, I really don't think that they're being helped while doing therapy through a screen. Just like as a teacher, I would be a much better if I were back in the classroom with them and breathing the same air.

∷∷∷∷∷
∷∷∷∷∷

I'll ask if they want to go back in person or continue working from home and invariably they all say, "I want to go back to school. I want to see my friends." As someone who has suffered from mental illness, I loved being alone; sometimes that exacerbates the whole problem. They talk about the end as being able to see their friends again, being able to go home. They want more contact with the outside world, which I think is a good sign.

There's something about looking at their body language that makes me so happy to be at [inpatient facility] right now. They're my students. When I'm with them, they can ask me questions, and I can tell stupid dad jokes. We're just inhabiting the same space, and I think it helps them. I can't say that it helps them therapeutically; that's a little bit presumptuous of me. It's really nice to just talk to students again because I haven't been able to for a long time. It helps my mental health when I'm with them.

Unfortunately, mental health is very unpredictable. Way too frequently, I hear in follow-ups that [kids aren't] doing so well. We're not working miracles over there. We do the best we can. We make sure that there's something stable, at least on paper or someone verbally assuring us, "Yeah, we got this. We'll take care of them when they get home."

But if they go home and they don't have something, then a lot of the time it falls apart. The people you think are going to be OK oftentimes aren't. And the ones you're like, "Oh, this kid's dead in the water when he gets home," turns out he's doing great. Dealing with young people with mental illness is really sad, but it's the most meaningful job I've ever had in my life.

I've been a better teacher since having kids, but in the residential treatment facility, I'm finding ways that I haven't really been a great father. Sometimes [the chef] isn't there on Mondays, so I cook them breakfast since I'm the one who gets there early. Today, I cooked them cheesy scrambled eggs, bacon, and diced fruits. And I thought at some point, *I don't do this for my own kids*. I'm finding that I'm extra sensitive about making sure that these kids are happy. And then my kids are at home with my wife, and I don't know what they're doing.

I need to cook breakfast for my kids tomorrow. I need to do something for them because I've been doing this for others all week.

I love waking up at five o'clock [to go to work]. I couldn't say that with my last job. I'm finally doing something meaningful at age 50. Not to say that teaching all those years wasn't meaningful. I've just been teaching a lot of privileged people for a long time, and now to see young people in absolute pain has really affected me.

But at the same time, I love it. Maybe I love it for selfish reasons. I just love getting up in the morning. I can't wait to get there and be an important person in someone's life. I don't have to be anything special other than someone who shows up every day and gives them their personalized daily agenda. I'm just keeping it simple, and it's making my life a lot nicer. If I can, all I need to be is this stable force for them. I keep thinking, *If I can be, all I need to be is this*.

— DESIRAE BROOKS

Hagerman—newly vaccinated—
was looking forward to an outdoor lunch with
the Restore Justice program director.
He was animated and eager to share his story,
even as we discussed some of
the difficulties of his past.

A Beacon of Hope

HAROLD HAGERMAN, APPRENTICE AT RESTORE JUSTICE ILLINOIS

When Harold Hagerman was 17 years old, he was tried as an adult and sentenced to sixty-one years in prison for aggravated battery and murder. While incarcerated at Menard Correctional Center[21] in southern Illinois, he earned his GED and an associate's degree, graduating from Hill Correctional Center[22] with a 4.0 GPA. Hagerman also completed life skills and reentry programs.

After serving twenty-eight years, Hagerman was released in April 2020. At the time of this interview, Hagerman had just reached the one-year anniversary of his release. He was living with his mother in Glenwood, Illinois,[23] as her primary caregiver and working as an apprentice for Restore Justice Illinois, a nonprofit focused on compassionate criminal-justice reform. He hoped that sharing his experiences could help other young men navigate the challenges he faced before, during, and after incarceration.

As we spoke on one of the first sunny, seventy-degree days of 2021, Hagerman—newly vaccinated—was looking forward to an outdoor lunch with the Restore Justice program director. He was animated and eager to share his story, even as we discussed some of the difficulties of his past.

IN THE BEGINNING, all you were seeing was the stories on the news. And by all accounts, it was like, "You catch this COVID thing, you get sick, and you die." That's how it was being delivered to us.

When it hit the prison system, it just ran through Stateville.[24] It was horrible, horrendous. We were seeing this stuff on the news, and we're seeing the numbers rise. We saw so many guys going to the hospital that they can't even hold them all, and people are dying by the hundreds. So naturally, we're scared to death.

The state map is showing these different counties, right? And each county might start at zero. The next day, they get three, and so on and so forth. And ours remained zero for quite some time, until it said one. Then the next day, it

---

[21] An Illinois state prison located in the town of Chester. It houses maximum-security and high medium-security adult males. It is the state's largest prison. Source: https://www2.illinois.gov/idoc/facilities/Pages/menardcorrectionalcenter.aspx

[22] A medium-security prison in Galesburg, Illinois.

[23] A village in Cook County about twenty miles south of Chicago.

[24] A maximum-security state prison for men in Crest Hill, Illinois, just outside Chicago.

said three. Through that process, a lot of us learned the meaning of "exponentially." We were very familiar with that term. We knew that this thing was coming, and it seemed to leave nothing untouched. When [it] hit us, they locked the facility down.

Early on, they weren't taking the situation seriously. The COs[25] weren't wearing a mask. They were joking about it. They would sneeze and cough as a joke because they knew how scared we were by the COVID thing. Just to freak us out. And being in there, there's no form of social distancing. It's, like, impossible, the social distancing in there. You're in there with your cellmate, you share a vent with the people next door, you're going outside into the day room, you're all using the same phones, you're using the same showers. It was really tough, man.

I was super concerned because I was coming home. I knew that you could be asymptomatic, so I didn't know if I had it. I don't know if my cellmate had it, and I was on the verge of coming home. I was concerned because my mother's up in age. I was concerned about coming home and—God forbid—getting her sick.

I'm begging them to test me, like, "Man, can I please get tested? I'm about to go home."

And it's, "No, we don't do that. We only test if you have new symptoms so severe that we're pretty sure it's COVID."

And I'm like, "Man, can you please tell them I'm about to go home? I don't want to risk getting my mom sick. I got all these concerns." And it was like, "No."

Their process was: if you develop any symptoms, cold-like symptoms, they just put you on quarantine, wait, and monitor you. And that's it. That was the test. Like, if you're sick to the point where they got to roll you up out of there, there's a chance you got COVID. If you get better, there you go. That was pretty much the test. You didn't get tested unless you was about to be put on a respirator. So that was scary.

But [I had to] man up. I put my mask on. I had to leave, you know? I had to go home. The whole family ended up getting tested, and we all were negative. That was a sigh of relief, man, but it was a really scary time because all we knew was that it was definitely like, "If you catch it, there's a good chance you're not going to make it." The healthcare system in there is deplorable at best.

None of my close friends had it at the time, before I left, but all of them have had it since.

∴∵∴∵∴∵
∵∴∵∴∵∴∵
∴∵∴∵∴∵

I had a pretty solid support system [growing up]. The issue with me, I think, was that my dad passed when I was 11. He was in Vietnam, and he came home really messed up. He was a good student, played drums in church, never did a day in the street. Just a really good, stand-up kid. He got drafted into the military. He got over there and saw some things no kid should ever see and experienced some things that traumatized [him]. When I grew up, there was a little turmoil during that period because he was struggling with psychological problems. I did witness some domestic violence and things of that nature in the house and home. Fast-forward some years, he ended up committing suicide.

My mom had to raise me and my sister on her own. My mom is originally from Englewood,[26] which is not a good area. It's really rough-and-tumble, but she went to school, to college. She did everything she had to do to make a better life for her children. She did a damn good job of it. I learned a lot from her. She was working, like, three jobs, so she wasn't able to be home and be as present, but she was hands-on and tried to stay on top of everything to the best of her abilities.

But, you know, kids, man. I didn't have my dad and I'm sad. I just... I don't know. My father passed, and I don't know, something changed. Prior to that, I was [getting], like, all As, participating in all types of programs, all of the clubs, all that stuff. Then I got to high school and I just wanted to have fun and kind of hang out. I looked to all the wrong people for influence, for guidance. That's how things went awry.

Me being young and impressionable, I just wanted to fit in with the cool crowd. I had cousins that were on the street that were tough guys. They were cool. They had all the nice clothes and the ladies. I looked up to them, so I was already familiar with that element, but I was too young to take part. When I got to high school, I was able to hang with these other guys. It was like, "These are my peers now. I can hang with these guys and they accept me. These are my friends."

They were gang affiliated. We started having problems with guys from another area, but it wasn't like gang banging or things of that nature. This was more of us protecting our neighborhood, right? It was like, we didn't want anything to happen to anybody over there. When kids were playing in the park or something, we'd tell them, "It's a lot going on right now. You guys go home." It was things of that nature. It was mostly like getting into fights and stuff like that.

But one day, it took a turn. A friend of mine named Wayne was, by all accounts, a good kid. It's important to note that he wasn't in the gang. He was a basketball player. That's what distinguished him from the rest of the guys that were around. He had a scholarship. He was about to go to IU,[27] I believe.

This is over the summer. He was preparing to go to college. One day he was up there playing basketball. We had left, me and my friends, to go to the store. I said,

---

[26] Englewood: A neighborhood in the South Side of Chicago.
[27] IU: Indiana University. At the time of Wayne's murder in 1993, IU's Division I basketball team had just won the Big Ten Conference and advanced to the NCAA Tournament's Elite Eight.

"We'll be right back." We left and when we got back, I noticed that the ambulance was in front of the park. I knew that a lot had been going on in the neighborhood as of recent, but nothing real crazy. I told my men I knew something was wrong. When we got up to the park, Wayne was lying there dead.

What happened was, the guys we were having back-and-forth issues with called some guy from another neighborhood to come over there and help them with the problem that they was having with us. They didn't come to fight. They came with weapons.

It was—it just—to just destroy this man's life, everybody was kind of, you know, just traumatized by that. Wayne was the one that was supposed to make it. A good, great kid. And, you know, all of us? We weren't bad kids. We were misunderstood.

That was a pivotal moment. It changed everything. I distinctly recall feeling so many different emotions, like so much anger and pain and hurt and fear and all these things at once, and it's too much for my teenage mind to process.

We came to the conclusion that we had to seek a form of justice. We didn't trust the police. We didn't trust the system when it came to justice, so we sought out street justice. And unfortunately, we found it.

All we could think was revenge or retaliation. That was the only thing we figured would make us feel better about the situation. This was a justifiable cause, in my crazy, teenage, young kid thinking. I wanted to protect my friends. That was basically the gist of it, and in the process of seeking revenge, another life was lost.

I was initially sent to the Cook County Jail. That's where I fought my case as well as the trial. Then I was sent to Menard Correctional Center, a.k.a. "The Pit." The end of the road. It's one of the prisons that's as far south as you can go in the state. If you come in from anywhere in the Chicagoland area, that's the one place you don't want to go, because your chance of getting visits and things of that nature is pretty slim. It is scary to pull up to that place. It looks like a prison you see in the movies. It's not as bad internally, but outside, it looks just like that.

[It's a misconception] that we're just in an empty cell with bars and a hole in the floor, curled up in a corner shivering. This is not that type of situation. You got TVs and electronics and appliances and commissary and cool cellmates, most times. I'm not saying it's a cake walk; I'm not saying you're living the dream. But it's just not as dismal and dark. It's not just a predator/prey type situation every day when you wake up. It's not like that.

I participated in a lot of different reentry programs and lifestyle redirection, behavior modification programs. I took anger management. I took a class called "Thinking for a Change." I took another one called "Start Now" that's just about changing your thought process from the person that you were coming in, to the person that you are now, and the person that's going home and reentering society. They prepare you for a lot of this stuff.

I was working in the correctional industries too, in the meat-processing plant. By all accounts for prison standards, it's like a real job. It's one of the best jobs you can have working in the correctional industry. You punch in and punch out on the clock, and you get real paychecks and all that type of stuff. You learn some transferable skills.

I was able to accumulate two years of "good time," which is basically good conduct credits, if that makes sense. I participated in a lot of those programs before it was incentive-based. That was just part of my rehabilitative efforts. I just wanted more for myself, and I wanted to prepare myself for the future.

∷∷∷∷∷••••
•∷∷∷∷••••

I met some of my best friends in prison. Those are some of my closest friends now, including the program director of Restore Justice. We were cellmates. We were best friends. Wendell Robinson, he's our program director.

Robinson was the first apprentice at the organization. With him going through the program directly under the executive director, he was able to carve out his own space, to carve out his own role and get on staff at the organization. After him, another guy followed, who is now the program associate at Restore Justice.[28]

These are my friends. I knew about the organization through them. Wendell had made me familiar with the program, and I told him I was on board. It was perfect. It allowed me to work in this space and to give back and help the people—my comrades—that I left behind. To be a beacon of hope for them, to fight for them and to work for them, and to keep them abreast [of] what's changed, what policies are in place, what deals are being pushed, what laws can possibly go into effect that might change their situations.

I'm part of the Future Leaders Apprenticeship Program. It allows returning citizens like myself—who have a commitment to social justice issues and a potential to impact the nonprofit sector—it allows us the opportunity to engage, to use our skills and passions for social good, to take on leadership roles in those areas. This program is really, really important and, as of right now, Restore Justice is the only organization that offers it.

VIRUS CITY

---

28 Nelson Morris, whose narrative appears on page 63.

Restore Justice is a 501(c)(4)[29] which allows them to go into politics and things of that nature. It puts me in a position to just be highly informed and to learn about advocacy and legislation. They go to Springfield and talk to legislators personally and lobby for bills to be passed. They draft up bills and bring their own stuff to the table and talk to legislators about things that can impact the system in a positive way. They create parole opportunities for people. They're highly involved in the juvenile justice system too, in terms of fair sentencing, justice, and equity.

I'm working on developing a project where I basically host a series of interviews of system-impacted individuals like myself, who are making significant strides in this space and doing this work in the social justice realm. It's highlighting and showcasing the accomplishments and achievements of returning citizens who have come home and hit the ground running. They're doing magnificent things in terms of social justice and criminal justice reform and reentry and mentoring programs. I believe that those stories need to be told, what can be achieved when given a second chance.

This organization is built on second chances, and it fights hard to fix this broken system. I want to do everything in my power to contribute to that, and to forward the agenda of Restore Justice. This is home for me.

....
....
....

[I was released] April 29 of 2020. How do you put that first day into words? It was exhilarating.

In a weird way, I was prepared. I didn't have a lot of the anxiety that you hear about. I was fully prepared to come home. I just walked out of the gate and I was, like, free.

The most standout moment, though? The first day I came home, they took me to Walmart. That was a memorable experience. They have so many options. This is a crazy sensory overload. I can't even—woo! I can't even explain it. You get in there, and you have no idea what to do first. What size you wear, what you like, what you don't like. It's like, "I like everything. Look at this stuff!"

We always joke among each other, like when guys come home or they're about to come home: "You got to take him to Walmart first. You got to take him." It's a thing now. It's a hell of an experience. And just being out here now, it's so normalized. You take things like that for granted, but to come home and just see that, it's like everything is just here at your disposal. It's a beautiful thing.

That was the first day. Seeing my mom, I got emotional because she was at home. I didn't want her to travel to come pick me up with the pandemic [because] we

[29] 501(c)(4): An organization exempt from federal income taxes under section 501(c)(4) of Title 26 of the United States Code. Unlike a 501(c)(3), a 501(c)(4) may engage in political advocacy and lobbying. Source: https://www.irs.gov/pub/irs-tege/eotopici03.pdf

would be in such a small space in the car. I hadn't been tested, and I knew you could be asymptomatic. I didn't want to chance, you know, with my ride back in that little space. When we got home, we hugged a little bit, and I got a little emotional.

Seeing my family, seeing how big and tall my niece had gotten—I've been imprisoned since she was born—seeing my family and a couple of my friends and being able to hug them—because of the pandemic, it was a little scary. We had a mask and stuff, but you can't social distance if you haven't been free with these people in almost thirty years. You picking them up and swinging them around and doing this whole thing. That was fun.

It was just an awesome feeling to be home after all that time and see how much the world had changed. It was a completely different world, even from what you're familiar with, the areas you're familiar with, from your old stomping grounds or surroundings or buildings or landmarks or shopping malls that have either expanded or gone. A lot of stuff is gone, and a lot [has been] built over that stuff. I was wide-eyed about the whole situation.

I wouldn't change anything in terms of being able to come home two years early, but I would have liked not to come home during a pandemic. It was like something out of a movie, man. It was really crazy, almost like the apocalypse. Imagine me coming home from prison and welcomed to this big world that is full of these endless possibilities, like, "Hey, man!" But it was like crickets, like, "Man, you go get in the house. What are you doing?"

I couldn't really celebrate my release the way you typically would. There was no big party, no social gatherings, none of that. There was no pomp and circumstance that probably could have surrounded me coming home after almost thirty years.

Now, I'm trying to do all the right stuff and am just putting every effort into becoming a law-abiding, productive member of society. I love, love, love life and love freedom. And I'm happy to be home. It's a welcome change of pace. It's quiet. It's a long way from prison, I tell you that.

— KAYLA SPENCER

Working at the restaurant for ten, eleven hours then coming home smelling like oil... the combination of long work hours and difficult school curriculum have really taken a toll on me mentally and physically.

Perpetual Motion

STEVEN, COLLEGE STUDENT

Steven is a 20-year-old college student studying at University of Illinois-Chicago (UIC) and working part time at his family's Chinese restaurant on the weekends. The COVID-19 pandemic has set a new course for the rest of Steven's life.

Steven told us of his experience being Asian in the pandemic, the current heated political climate, and about widespread misinformation encountered by his family and many others.

IT IS WEDNESDAY. I wake up, look at my phone, brush my teeth, eat lunch, go to school online, help my dad fill out some documents, watch the news, eat dinner, play some games, and go to bed. It is Thursday. I wake up, look at my phone, brush my teeth, skip lunch, go to school online, wonder where my sister is, eat dinner, read some news, and go to bed. It is Friday. I wake up, look at my phone, brush my teeth, go to work as a delivery driver at my family restaurant, watch the news all day, eat dinner, come home, and knock out. It is Saturday. I repeat Friday.

Every day I really wonder when this will end. Every day feels the same, and it is driving me to a point of silent insanity.

How did this all happen? Before the pandemic, honestly not everything was amazing, but life was enjoyable, you know? I was an engineer at UIC. Grades were OK, not terrible. I had a social life where my friends and I would play volleyball often at the student rec center. My roles were mainly setter and libero, but I can flex into anything. Afterwards, my friends and I would often get food together. We loved Korean BBQ and sushi especially. I still worked weekends at my family's restaurant, but nothing felt out of control. Everything was manageable.

Then the lockdown just hit us all of a sudden.

The transition from physical to online school was very drastic. A lot of the classes really weren't prepared, and neither was I.

I have classes online Monday to Thursday, and [I] work Friday to Sunday now. I have not seen friends or grandparents in months. Working at the restaurant for ten, eleven hours then coming home smelling like oil... the combination of long work hours and difficult school curriculum have really taken a toll on me mentally and physically.

I [can't] just quit my job and focus on school. My family doesn't want to hire another delivery driver 'cause they prefer to work with family, and I don't get an allowance. So, yeah.

Honestly, I didn't think that online school would be difficult when it started, but boy, was I wrong. Moving from classroom to Zoom completely messed up my ability to keep track of assignments and lectures. Also, some of my classes, like Calculus 2, felt like I was literally teaching myself everything. In fact, I changed my major from engineering to business because I couldn't handle the engineering curriculum online.

The only people I interact with now are the customers at the restaurant. But frankly, I'm tired of that too, since sometimes I have to pretend to be nice to certain people despite them being rude.

My family closed the restaurant for about three weeks, and it affected us heavily since we are not that well off. We had to open back up immediately with safety precautions whenever we could. The unemployment benefits really helped us through the closing, and I helped my family sign up for all of them because they didn't know how.

At work, I sometimes watch the front as a cashier, sometimes answering the phone for takeout orders, but my main job is a delivery boy. Nothing has changed much at the restaurant except masks and more safety measures. The same customers still come. Business hasn't gone down or up really, and the delivery tips mostly stayed the same.

But there were a couple interesting new customers that came in. The first interesting customer was an older person who looked like a veteran. It was during the middle of the pandemic, and he saw us and other customers wearing masks. He was also wearing a mask, but I suspect it was just to follow the restaurant's rules. He was just kind of speaking to himself out loud about how COVID was a conspiracy and that the news and feds are feeding us lies. That the vaccine is just here to control us. Everybody in the restaurant sort of just ignored him since he wasn't being hostile and just trying to provoke reactions. He got his food and he left without causing too much of a scene.

The second one was wearing a MAGA[30] hat. I'm usually pretty indifferent to a person's political beliefs unless they act out, but I do have some biases. He started speaking about the virus and of us being Chinese. At first, I was appalled and just thinking like, *Here we go again*.

But he surprised me. He was trying to be genuinely nice and said to me, "I know you guys hear so many bad things like that—'oh, it's a Chinese virus,' or 'you guys brought it from China.' I just want you to know, not everybody thinks that way. Don't stress about it." It was very comforting hearing that, especially coming from a Trump supporter. I was glad that someone told me he didn't blame all of us.

But still, what changed the most for me was definitely people's attitude towards the Asian-American community. The pandemic really [shone] a light at our community and the problems affecting us. Every day you would hear some news about crimes happening to Asian Americans and even in Chinatown. It is very disheartening.

I have an uncle that manages a grocery store in Chinatown and there was an incident there where an African American went into the store and was harassing some of the customers. He was asked to leave but got aggressive and attacked one of the workers, who threatened to call the police. It actually made the news and went a little viral on social media. My uncle who runs the store used to be a cop, so he had the experience to take him down and held him until the police arrived. The victim had some bruising. I'm not sure what happened to the aggressor. The rest of my family heard about this story soon, and they were pretty encouraged by the fact that not all Asians will just stand there and do nothing when they get harassed or attacked.

We pretty much grew up in Chinatown and spent lots of time there. Nowadays, our senior citizens and grandparents can't even go out anymore without feeling uncomfortable in their own hometown where their people are. So, I feel like it's our duty to protect them.

As for my own personal experiences, I didn't face any physical violence. The worst I experienced was when I was walking down the street and this lady walking her dog saw me and said, "Don't eat my dog" under her breath.

Right as the first batch of vaccines were coming, my mom was pretty skeptical. I know they were more scared of the virus than the vaccine at first. She objected to it for a while before I convinced her. It wasn't hard to convince her; it was more of

---

[30] The slogan "Make America Great Again" and its acronym, MAGA, was adopted by the Donald J. Trump campaign for president, often appearing on a red baseball cap. Source: https://www.washingtonpost.com/politics/how-donald-trump-came-up-with-make-america-great-again/2017/01/17/fb6acf5e-dbf7-11e6-ad42-f3375f271c9c_story.html

an inevitably. She wanted to be able to go out again, go shopping, see my grandma, and protect her, so the pros outweighed the cons.

At first, she saw all these articles on WeChat, a popular Chinese messaging app, and some of them said the vaccine had a chance to give her a numb face. Some of the stuff you find on WeChat is very akin to anti-vaxxers. There's a lot of misinformation in that area.

Like, I don't understand why vaccines have to be political, either. I feel like people should listen to science instead of choosing to get vaccinated based on your political stance. It's pretty frustrating. I'm kind of upset at the fact that we have been stuck in a pandemic for so long. If Donald Trump [had taken] it more seriously and encouraged vaccines and masks earlier, we would have saved more lives. I would be out of this cycle of nothingness sooner.

Speaking of Trump again... Unlike me, my parents actually prefer him over Biden, although they don't vote because they can't miss a day of work. Their reasoning was that they see all these news articles about people committing crimes in the name of George Floyd and breaking in stores and robbing them and stuff. They see this stuff and think, like, *Oh, it's because California is run by Democrats, so that's why there's so much crime happening there.* They think that a Republican running the place results in the crime being handled better.

Frankly, I understand both sides. I feel that peaceful protest doesn't get news coverage or a strong response, but some people are just out there rioting to riot or stealing, and it hurts their cause. A lot of these people don't understand African American struggles or sentiment. So, I can see how my parents are spoon fed this narrative, but I can also see that some rioters took advantage of this situation.

There is bad blood between the Asian and African American communities for sure. The pandemic, riots, and crime news definitely made it worse. My parents even want to move out of the city and go to Texas since they want to see [fewer] African Americans, but I told them that they will just face other problems like racist white people. Asians and African Americans have their own different sets of struggles. African Americans get treated differently because of their skin color and face more police brutality than others. Like, they can't even walk down the street without being threatened or sometimes shot at by the police.

Us Asians, the police don't generally bother us, but people see us as non-threatening, like somebody to be made fun of or taken advantage of. And watching the news, we definitely get taken advantage of, especially our most vulnerable elderly.

Despite everything, I believe that unity will be our greatest strength going forward. From MAGA-hatters to African Americans to us, what we all need is to give each other a chance. The best way to do it is to just stop stereotyping. Both sides have common stereotypes of each other, and that just makes them vulnerable to racial slurs and negativity. If everybody sees each other as an individual, then maybe that'll be a step towards ending this hostility.

COVID may have put a spotlight on many bad things, but it is in that light where hope for a more united future can be found. To end this perpetual cycle of generational hostility between all the groups of people starts with you and me.

It is Sunday. I wake up, get out of my bed, brush my teeth, and enjoy my life and its bright future to the fullest.

— JIMMY CHEN

As we began our conversation, Greene apologized for the noise her cat was making as it meowed and scratched her closed door.

Thrown to the Sharks

"SARAH GREENE," TEACHER

Sarah Greene (a pseudonym) is a 23-year-old first-year teacher at a religious private school in Chicago. During her first year of student teaching in Chicago Public Schools (CPS), the pandemic abruptly cut off her experience, so she has had to adjust the way she approaches being a brand-new teacher. She moved to the private school in August 2020.

At the time of this interview in early February 2021, the Chicago Teachers' Union and CPS were battling over when and how to reopen schools to allow K-8 students back in the classroom.[31] As we began our conversation, Greene apologized for the noise her cat was making as it meowed and scratched her closed door.

[IN 2020], I WAS STUDENT TEACHING in CPS at a school on the North Side, a K through 8 cluster magnet school. It was a fairly normal student-teaching experience until the pandemic hit in March. It was supposed to be a full year, from August of 2019 until the end of the 2020 school year. That week of March 9 through March 14, I was in the middle of my full takeover. [That's] when you don't just teach random lessons with the mentor teacher supporting you, but the mentor teacher will take a step back and let you take over the classroom fully for four weeks.

That Tuesday, we went on a field trip with the kids to a museum. They were second-graders, and they were all, "Am I going to get the coronavirus?" We were like, "No. It's fine." They had their little hand sanitizers with them, and we weren't wearing masks. That's all of what we knew. We had no idea that one week later, everything would be gone.

No one had a plan. The leadership in CPS didn't have a plan for the district, and the school didn't really have a plan, either. We did what we could to support our mentor teachers. The communication was hard. No one was used to this Zoom world yet.

When we started doing online school for student teaching, I started to notice certain students would never show up. Those were the students who had to be bused to the

31 Source: https://www.nytimes.com/2021/02/07/us/chicago-schools-open-coronavirus.html

school from very far away, who were from low-income families, who didn't have internet access. They really didn't get to finish second grade. We would do weekly Zoom calls to check in with the kids, and videos of lessons would get uploaded to Google Classroom. So there were some students who didn't have access to school at that point.

At the very beginning, once everything shut down, we still had this sense of hope. "Oh, if we just stay home for two weeks, we're going to beat this." I had some hope for a little while. But after I started to sit at home for weeks and weeks, I was like, "What am I supposed to do?" Our professor wants us to do one thing, my mentor teacher wants us to do another. There is no clear communication. That is sort of when I realized, *Oh, crap. This is real. This is really happening.*

Our graduation ceremony was canceled. I had been really looking forward to that since I was in high school. It meant a lot for me to graduate, so once we hit that lull a few weeks into the quarantine phase, and that ceremony was canceled, and everything else started to get canceled, I started to realize, What am I going to do? *What is next year going to look like? I have no idea.* No one really knew what the classroom would look like.

That was the scariest part: *How am I going to teach in a mask? How are the kids going to spread out? Are they going to listen?* So, I didn't really get to see in-person learning until I was thrown to the sharks.

• • • • • • • •
• • • • • • • • • • •
• • • • • • • • •

I worked at a summer camp [in the] summer of 2020. [I] was hopeful because it was outdoors, and we were told that being outdoors was much safer, but we still had to follow tons of rules: only ten kids in a group, groups can't mingle, scan every kid's temperature when they arrive. We all acted like we knew what we were doing because we had all these CDC[32] guidelines, but obviously we didn't.

One of the days, we were preparing how we were going to welcome all these kids. The first day of camp is the first time these kids have been anywhere since school closed. We were trying on PPE[33] gear: [a] huge blue smock, [a] face shield, and an N95. I put it all on and I just burst into tears. I told my boss, "I cannot approach a child in their car like this. I can't do it."

I thought of myself at five years old, sitting in the back of the car. If a camp counselor rolled down my window and approached with that, I would have never come back. That speaks to the resiliency of this generation of kids, the fact that they're pushing through this. We're not giving them enough credit for it.

---

[32] Centers for Disease Control and Prevention, the U.S. health protection agency.
[33] Personal protective equipment

I struggled in college. I struggled in high school. I grew up going to a very small, community-based school where my teachers watched me grow up from kindergarten through eighth grade. A teacher is with you not just academically but emotionally. Then I went to a huge public high school of four thousand students where I felt like my teachers didn't care about me, and that changed my attitude, which stuck with me through college. It was sort of like, *These professors don't care about me as a human.*

I think the experience that really drew me to teaching happened in high school. I was really involved in spoken-word poetry, and I started getting involved in poetry slams in the city.

[One] poetry slam [did] a kickoff event—I think it was called Crossing the Street—where every single team from every school would come to one high school and fill up the auditorium. Kids from the city, kids from the suburbs, all different kinds of teenagers would come together and get to know each other. They would put kids from different schools in groups and have them talk about their life experiences and get to know each other.

Something that I really focus on in my teaching is social and emotional learning. I think that unless you are emotionally secure and socially safe, you cannot learn. I thought that spoken word was a great way for young people to express how they felt. It made me realize, *Wow, when I grow up, these young people will be my students.*

A lot of the poetry that young people were sharing [at the poetry slam] was about school, and about how they were experiencing things at home, certain traumas that stopped them from being able to succeed, how their teachers would get on them for it and didn't understand them. They weren't trying to be disrespectful. They were just struggling. You don't know what's happening in the student's life, so let's try to unpack it so that they can learn. It changed who I was and made me a more open-minded person and a better teacher.

My school now is a religious private school, where I teach fifth grade. We opened in person in August [2020]. It was challenging, especially at the beginning. Once I figured out who my students are, it made it easier.

There's a lot of discourse out there about virtual learning and how it's damaging for kids. I want to push back against that a little bit because there are students who thrive with online learning. They get to be in, and control, their own space.

I think [others] are going to be traumatized because of the way [in-person] school is this year. Behind shields, with all of these restrictions, they feel like they're trapped in a box.

It's important, letting them know that it's OK to struggle with remote learning and it's also OK [if they're] not. I think a lot of the attitude among the kids is, "This sucks! We want to be back in person, in school." But there are kids who are like, "What if I don't? What if I like having my space and having remote learning and like being at home? What if that's where I feel safe?" It's helpful just letting them know that it's OK to struggle with in-person learning with all the rules, and it's also OK to struggle [with] learning at home. There's no right or wrong way to learn during this pandemic.

I'm a substitute permanently in the building so that they don't have to call random subs and expose more people all the time. I've been doing a lot of maternity-leave positions, so I have been having my own students. I really like to allow my students to be creative, even if it's outside of the curriculum. I try to do things like, "Let's talk about what a good learning environment looks like, and let's write about it." I also like to try to figure out who my students are and use that to my advantage. To their advantage, really.

I had a student who struggled a lot in class. He struggled to pay attention and not shout out random, goofy things. I figured out that he's a really techy kid. He loves technology, and I could use that and let him do his work using the technology that he loves. He really loves to be in his own special space and be a leader. That helped him stay focused and learn. I think it's just looking at a kid as a kid, and a whole child, before they are a student.

· · · · · · · ·
· · · · · · · · · · · ·
· · · · · · · · · ·

At the beginning, I was obviously hesitant to go to work in person, but I could tell with all the restrictions they were putting in place that the [private] school had the money to open safely. CPS just didn't. [In 2020] I was at was one of the CPS schools that was more funded than other CPS schools are, but at the same time, there were bathrooms and water fountains that didn't work. There wasn't a nurse. There were all of these inequities that were at play.

When the pandemic came around, all of those inequities really started to show. [CPS] didn't have the classroom sizes or the number of teachers necessary to open safely. At the private school, we have the desks spread six feet apart in the rooms, and the desks have shields on all of them, which are expensive. We have a medical advisory board of doctors who are doing contact tracing. We have weekly testing for staff and students. There are fifteen kids or less in each classroom, [which] does not happen in CPS. In the school I was student teaching at, the kindergarten classroom had thirty-nine kids to one teacher. When I think about how CPS is pushing for reopening, I think about that kindergarten versus the classrooms with thirteen kids that I'm still struggling with and I think, "How is that even going to happen?"

Obviously [the private school] is expensive, and the students at my school are wealthier than a lot of students at public schools. They have internet access. If we have to say, "We have a couple cases at school, we have to go remote for the next two weeks," they can just, at the snap of a finger, go remote, because they have the resources.

Sometimes we go remote to be [cautious]. We went remote for a week after Thanksgiving break, winter break, just in case families decided to travel, which we can't control. It's a privilege to be able to do that, to be able to say, "OK, we're going to have a week of remote so that your family can do what they want over break." And even though we have all of these things, it's still hard.

Even though we are able to open safely because of all the resources that we have, all these other teachers and I are still struggling. When you take a group of ten 11-year-olds and you spread them out six feet apart in these desks, which ends up taking up the entire room, there are so many social barriers that get in the way of being able to teach like that. They don't get to sit at their tables and talk with their friends. It's exhausting for them to constantly be scolded and told to spread out and separate.

······
··············
········

I think having a community, making friends with the other teachers in the building, is a huge help. I know sometimes it can become toxic in teaching communities to just complain all the time and stew in negativity. But on the other side of that, I think having coworkers and other teacher friends to vent to is so helpful, to know that you're not alone.

When I talk to a teacher who has been teaching for ten years, and she tells me, "I feel like a first-year teacher this year," having that reassurance is very helpful, to know that it isn't me, that I'm not a bad teacher. [It's] teachers of all subjects, grades, experiences, who are struggling. I think having that connection is the best for my mental health.

The best part of this whole thing has been the kids, and the connections, for sure. One hundred percent. It makes me want to cry, just them and their resiliency. It's causing me to reflect a lot on who I was as a kid. Would we have been able to handle this?

I'm just amazed. I tell them all the time, but it's hard for them to understand because they don't know what it's like to be an adult and look back on a normal elementary school experience. I don't think they even realize how resilient they've been.

I didn't think it would be possible to connect with them through the computer, or with masks on, without them even knowing what I look like. But it is possible. There's so much that you can tell about a person from their eyes and from their body language. It's made me amazed that we were able to do this.

[The kids] are going to talk about this forever. When they grow up, there's going to be kids who were in school in person the whole time, there's going to be kids who were stuck in their bedroom for ten, twelve months. They're going to have a lot of discourse comparing those experiences, and I think that's going to be a huge part of their teen and adult years. I don't really know how to explain it in the way that I want to, but I think that this is going to be what defines this generation.

— JENNA SHATTUCK

You Need to Giggle

LAURA, NURSE

Laura is a 58-year-old nurse at Northwestern Memorial Hospital in Chicago. She works primarily with outpatients who have gastrointestinal issues, preparing them for procedures. She has been at Northwestern since 2013, but she has worked in various hospital settings since the late '80s.

The majority of this conversation took place just after a February 2021 cold snap. The previous week was characterized by heavy snowfall. Laura said that the day before the first interview, she was a "noodle," having gotten up at 3:45 a.m. to make the forty-mile drive to work.

At the beginning of the conversation, Laura recruited technology help from Kelsey, one of her daughters, who is 16. While Hilary, 14, another daughter, tried on some of Laura's rings in another part of the bedroom, a cat meowed offscreen. Throughout the interview, family members came in to ask Laura questions. A crucifix hung on the wall behind her.

HOW LONG HAVE I BEEN A NURSE? 1986. But I took like nine years off after I had my kids, and then I went back part time. I worked full time until then. I have a huge, colorful, gigantic history of nursing.

It's a good little job. I find it very valuable. It's a total commitment to colon cancer screening. You talk about people's poop and pee, all the farting and gas and stuff like that. The physicians that I work with, they're so much fun. They're completely laid-back people because all they do is talk about that stuff with you.

I admitted this boy— It wasn't a boy, he's like a 32-year-old man. He was six-foot-three. His feet were hanging off the end of the cart. He was probably 250 pounds. I opened up his chart and I'm like, this guy's been here for three months. He's got [COVID]. He had been intubated and then got a trach.[34]

If you're going to be on a ventilator for a long time, they trach you because it's just too much on your mouth to have that intubation tube. But he had several revisions

---

[34] A tracheotomy, in which the trachea or windpipe is surgically opened to provide airflow to and from the lungs.

of his trach, and he had—this is crazy—a suture going through his chin to his chest wall so that his head would stay extended. If he moved his head back this much, it would occlude his airway, so they stitched his chin to his chest to keep his head stable so he could always breathe. All he was doing was coming down for an airway check.

I asked him about his emotional stress. And he just started to cry. Every patient that comes in now, we have to do a psychosocial screening on them. We have to ask them if their home life is safe, if they're being abused in any way, are they suicidal? Do they want to see a chaplain? Do they have any specific religious needs that we need to [attend to]? Mostly that's screening out Jehovah's Witnesses because they don't take certain blood products. Everyone gets the psychosocial.

It was the most heartbreaking thing for him.

I've been a nurse so long, and when I went into nursing school in the '80s is not the way you practice nursing now, in this century. It's totally, totally changed. But I was completely overwhelmed, and the first thing I did was grab his hand and hold his hand, which was the basic nursing skill that I learned in the '80s. We spend so much time doing paperwork, and then this was just holding this individual's hand.

His aunt had died since he had been admitted, and it was an abrupt death. She had died from a cardiac arrest. I knew his aunt.

It was so strange. There was a Zoom memorial service that night, but it was just so hard on him because he had no way to say goodbye to her.

That was one of my later cases. That was in December [2020].

∷∷∷∷∷∷ ∙∙∙

I'm not dealing with the front lines. I just take care of patients who are already positive or, like that gentleman, he was just coming in to hopefully get that thing snipped off his chin. I have never seen anything like that in my life. I've been a nurse a long time, and that was just crazy.

I prepare people for colonoscopies and upper endoscopies and ERCPs.[35] I'm in an outpatient setting, so when the pandemic hit, that became a non-essential, elective procedure. We have a twelve-procedure room area that's all outpatients. They closed all that up.

I can't tell you how many patients are like, well, I was scheduled for this in April and it got canceled, and that was like the impact on the hospital. The nurses that are

---

[35] Endoscopic retrograde cholangiopancreatographies. Laura explained that an ERCP is an exploratory procedure that examines the biliary, liver, and pancreatic regions for blockages.

in the clinic have to start rescheduling people. And so they're making hundreds of phone calls, trying to get people back on track.

We were so behind in all those cases—it must have been August, September, October [of 2020]—we were doing 150 procedures a day. It was awful.

I think it took us 'til about the middle of December to get caught up. Then things started to lighten up a little bit, and then somebody would get COVID, and they'd be gone for two weeks.

All that staff had to be redispersed in the hospital too. A lot of the CRNAs, which are certified registered nurse anesthetists, they went back to the ICUs to work, and they haven't been in the ICU for a long time.

Elective surgeries, colonoscopies—that's a lot of money for a hospital. And the hospital lost a lot of money because they couldn't do them for four, five months. They paid us even though we weren't working. People who couldn't get another job for a while, they still got a paycheck no matter what.

But during that time, I worked a whole lot more hours. Everybody had to go out and find a new job. A lot of people went to the COVID hotline. A lot of people went to the COVID tent and started swabbing people. They would get busy in a day, or they would know that the next day they were going to be busy. My manager would call me and say, can you come in the next day?

During the time when COVID was really, really bad, they built almost a mini-ICU. It's a lot of beds, but they're individual beds with the sliding doors, as opposed to a regular floor room. And so they moved the non-COVID ICU patients in next door there so that all the COVID patients were up here.

And the only reason I mention that is because everyone had to disperse and go to different places. All the floors got closed. People had to find other places to work.

· · · · · · · ·
· · · · · · · · · · ·
· · · · · · · · · ·

We were fortunate. I work at a big major medical center, [but] they did make us save [our masks]. You would go to work, and then you'd save [your mask] in a brown paper bag so that when you came back to work the next day, you can use the same one. Sometimes you just sweat so much, you've got to get rid of 'em, you know?

I think in the beginning, they were so worried about running out of [PPE]. There were times that you'd go to the supply room and there'd be a whole different kind of glove there. It was very noticeable. We had these one kind of duckbill N95s that we loved, and then they just disappeared. We got these other ones that nobody liked to wear.

And you'd need to wear two[36]and a face shield,[37] the whole bit, and gown and glove. The people doing procedures had to put all that stuff on and then get in the room. You have to do it outside the room, just like you would in if you were in a hospital instead of in an outpatient setting.

I've swabbed about maybe three people now that have ended up being positive. One case that I did—two days later, I didn't feel good. They sent me home, and I got the COVID test, and it was negative.

My husband worked from home. He's very busy at the end of October and into November, and he had to go to work. He showed up, and he's just like, "I didn't feel good. My temperature was high."

When my husband called me at work and said, "I'm positive," they sent me home. And then I had to have another COVID test, and I couldn't work for fourteen days.[38] Now it's down to ten days. They've decreased the isolation time to being about ten days if you are negative, but your family member is positive.[39]

I slept on the couch for two weeks. I didn't get it. And my two girls didn't get it from him. And we all lived together. He had a very mild case. He was fine. He didn't have to get hospitalized.

I would come home from work and strip in the garage, put my clothes right in the washing machine, and I usually had a towel sitting right by the back door, and then go upstairs and take a shower when I got home from work for those first couple of months. You learn to live with it.

I'm a little less paranoid [now], and I understand the disease a little bit better. Like, I'm not afraid of it. I mean, I'm not really coming in contact now with people with COVID as much as you would think. And even then, I have something over [the clothes], something that's disposable. I'm not taking all my clothes off anymore because I feel safer with it.

---

[36] In an early 2021 interview with NBC's *Today*, Dr. Anthony Fauci, the president's chief medical advisor, expressed the opinion that wearing two masks instead of one "just makes common sense," as the doubling up could add extra layers of filtration and cover gaps. Source: www.webmd.com/lung/news/20210126/double-masking-makes-common-sense-fauci-says.

[37] A clear plastic barrier worn over the face to prevent the spread of droplets, especially to the eyes. See "Other Types of Face Protection" at www.cdc.gov/coronavirus/2019-ncov/prevent-getting-sick/cloth-face-cover-guidance.html.

[38] Self-quarantining, or avoiding outside contact for two weeks after a possible exposure to COVID-19, is meant to reduce the risk of unknowingly infecting others. Symptoms (fever, nausea, shortness of breath, etc.) are expected to develop within that time frame. Source: www.cdc.gov/coronavirus/2019-ncov/if-you-are-sick/quarantine.html.

[39] In late 2020, the Centers for Disease Control and Prevention allowed people living in the same household as a COVID-19-positive person to isolate for ten days rather than the previous fourteen as long as the other people in the household show no symptoms. Source: https://www.cdc.gov/coronavirus/2019-ncov/more/scientific-brief-options-to-reduce-quarantine.html

I'm very relaxed about it. Maybe too relaxed, I don't know. I still haven't gotten it. I've been exposed at least seven times and I have not gotten it between work and family and friends.

What I've learned over almost a year of this is that there's a way to live with it and to be smart about it. If you stay hidden all the time, it's not good for you either. Your mental status is just as important. I've seen my mother, who is elderly, and we've socially isolated her so much that she's just gotten more confused. She's in her 90s.

:::::::::

I yelled at two people about their masks, but I think that's pretty good in almost a year. They kind of roll their eyes at you. Like punky kids at Walmart. They were teenagers, holding their masks in their hand. Just put your mask on.

And then just the other day, I was at work. I got on the [parking garage] elevator at six, and I take it to three. On the fourth floor, we stopped, and two construction dudes got in, and one wasn't wearing a mask at all. He had his back towards me. I'm like, here's the sign right here. I read the sign. It said, "A mask is required in here."

They got off at three with me. There's a hand [sanitizer] station there and a mask station there, so you can get one right away. I finally turned around and I was just like, "You should have a mask on."

"Well, I didn't have one in my car."

I go, "But you were on an elevator with me and a shared space. It's a shared space. You need to have a mask on."

"Oh, well, I'm getting one on now."

I go, "That's a little too late." And I go, "You should have taken the stairs down."

One flight. One flight would have been all he would have had to do to take the stairs down.

I get it that you don't have a mask at the time. I get sometimes they fall out of your car when you get in and out, or they get dirty. I get that. But then, take the staircase down. You don't have to take the elevator. I think there's legitimately some people that have paranoia or they're claustrophobic and they can't handle the mask. You see people in a parking lot and they rip it off.

I wear a mask for a solid nine hours a day.

If you come to the hospital, let's say you have a made mask—you know, a hand-made one. They ask you take that off and put one of the hospital ones on. I'm constantly pinching the nose or making people cover up. If they're in the hospital, and it's the ride that's picking somebody up, I do not hesitate. I'm like, "Can you slip that [up]?" I'm always polite.

I don't want it. I don't want to give it to my kids. I'm sure there's just as many nurses that have elderly people at their home. I know this might sound bitchy, but we've just been dealing with it for so long and have learned to live with it, within the limitations of what we've got going on in our own homes. And yet we're still here and we're still doing it. There's no job that is more at risk than anybody else's, because we're all at risk for getting it and giving it to somebody else.

I don't think we're going to get rid of the masks for another year. I think we'll be going well into 2022 with the masks on. And I think it's effective. It's unbelievable that this flu season has been nothing because of [masking].

The only time we take our masks off is when we're having lunch. Sometimes there's only two of us at a table or we're sitting far apart. We've always been a community in the [gastrointestinal] lab. We go to lunch together. That's been another fallout from COVID—we can't sit, go outside and go for a walk together.

It's hard. You want to be with your friends and giggle with them. One of the reasons I work is for that social interaction. I love being a nurse and I take a lot of pride in it. But I do start to miss people.

∴∴∴∴∴∴∴
∴∴∴∴∴∴∴

I got my vaccinations in December [2020] and in January [2021].[40] That was through the hospital. I went on my lunch hour. I didn't have any trouble. It's kind of funny because I went to the gym those days after work, and one day I was doing arms, and I don't know if I just sweated it out or what. Some people get really, really sick from it, but I [had] no problem at all.

That's whole thing about COVID: anything could happen. It doesn't have to make any sense why some people get it, why some people don't, why some people have harder symptoms. Who would think that 32-year-old young man would have to be hospitalized for three months from COVID when my husband, who's 57, had a headache and fatigue and a fever for three days, and then was fine?

I have a really, really good friend. We went K-12 together. She has advanced MS[41] up to her shoulders. She got COVID. She got COVID bad.

40 The Pfizer and Moderna COVID-19 vaccines require administration in two doses. Source: www.cdc.gov/coronavirus/2019-ncov/vaccines/faq.html.
41 Multiple Sclerosis

She got intubated. They tried to extubate her; they made three attempts before they could do it. They had her in the ICU, and she was sedated the whole time. So she had no idea what was going on, right?

She woke when they got her off the ventilator one day. This is how she described it. She looked up, and she could see the look on her husband's face and on her 16-year-old daughter's face. And she goes, "Oh, I'm really sick. I must really, really be sick." [She] went home on oxygen.

Here's somebody who should have died of COVID, right? She didn't, and she fought it. She's a 58-year-old lady with advanced MS. She hasn't moved a muscle in I don't know how long. And she fought it, and she won.

I do think that there is a way to live with it and still have some sort of semblance of life. Get out and get your vaccine. People are really, really nervous about the vaccine. They don't want to get the vaccine because they think they're going to grow a third arm or whatever.

Even some people that have a lot of medical problems don't get [the vaccine]. And then you have your young adults that are getting [COVID]. We had a teenage girl, an 18-year-old girl, die. It was just devastating for a lot of people.

The frustration with trying to get the vaccine, that's the worst. I just was listening to NPR where this woman kept refreshing and refreshing [the vaccine appointment websites], and she couldn't get the vaccine.

My sister, who is over 65, she lives in California. She couldn't get the vaccine. She finally started looking to go during the time of the Super Bowl and got the vaccine. I couldn't get my 91-year-old mother in there. The hard part was signing up online. I signed my mother up for two places. I signed up through the hospital, and I signed her up through Cook County. And I finally heard from Cook County. But she's 91...

I think the vaccine's going to minimize your symptoms. It doesn't mean that you don't have to wear a mask and you don't have to social distance.

∙∙∙∙∙∙∙∙∙∙∙∙
∙∙∙∙∙∙∙∙∙∙∙∙∙

I really like [my job], and I really feel like I've done a lot with it. My kids listen to my stories. They must be interesting because they're so not interested in going into healthcare, but they'd like to hear the stories about the people that I meet every day.

I feel like it's kept us close. [To Hilary, off-screen] Don't you think that COVID's kept us close? Yeah. We comment about how we're the only family we know that spends so much time together.

I would say 99 percent of it is good. We've been watching mass on TV.[42] My husband and I were doing walks together. My kids have kind of the same sense of humor as my husband and me, and so we'll have Friday night movie nights. We would watch a scary movie. We did the whole *Annabelle* series. That was really fun.

My husband and I, we're older. We got married late. I have two teenage daughters. And I was like, you got to watch *Amityville Horror*. You got to watch horror shows from when I was a kid. So we kind of have done that. Hilary's making us watch *Criminal Minds*. So it's just kind of fun that way. They're not up in their bedrooms on their phones by themselves. They're downstairs in the family room with my husband and me.

What do you think, Hilary? We've spent a lot of time together, right? We watched all those movies, all those scary movies together. What else do we watch that we really enjoyed together? [*Criminal Minds*.] Yeah, see. I knew.

—ELIZABETH RUDA

42 Cardinal Blase Cupich suspended the celebration of public Masses in the Archdiocese of Chicago. Here, Laura refers to the broadcast of the Mass from Mercy Home for Boys and Girls. Later in 2021 parishes reopened under social-distancing guidelines. Source: https://www.archchicago.org/statement/-/article/2020/04/05/decree-cardinal-blase-j-cupich-archbishop-of-chicago-dispenses-the-faithful-from-easter-obligations

Nobody Can Take Away
That Voice

ÓSCAR SÁNCHEZ, DIRECTOR OF YOUTH AND
RESTORATIVE JUSTICE PROGRAMMING

Óscar Sánchez, 23, is the co-founder of the Southeast Youth Alliance (SYA) and Director of Youth and Restorative Justice Programming for Alliance of the Southeast (ASE), a coalition of churches, businesses, schools, and other community organizations. Sánchez has a history of activism, beginning with student government at Harold Washington College in Chicago, then with several other groups on the Southwest Side. He assisted in the organizing of Black Lives Matter (BLM) marches in the Southeast Side after the death of George Floyd in the summer of 2020, and in early 2021 conducted a thirty-day hunger strike to stop General Iron[43] from moving to the Southeast Side. General Iron recently closed its Lincoln Park location after years of complaints about pollution and poor air quality.

The day before this interview in May 2021, Mayor Lori Lightfoot delayed the permit process for General Iron after the federal government expressed concerns about environmental damage.[44] On February 18, 2022, the Chicago Department of Public Health denied the permit.[45]

WE ARE AT A POINT where people feel like things are getting back to normal. What I tell people when they're saying things are going back to normal is that you don't understand how much privilege you have, because there are people's homes being taken away at this moment. We have people being evicted even though there's these laws that say no eviction.[46] We have gentrification happening in the Southwest [Side]. Families are struggling [while] people say things are getting back to normal. If "normal" is people being oppressed, then I don't want it.

[2020] really shined a light on what's always been there. [Our] community is always the first to be dying, and it's not right, so we fight because we deserve more than this. We deserve more than to have our lives and our homes sacrificed for the rich, for profit. We are human beings.

---

43 General Iron Industries Inc. owned and operated a metal shredding and recycling operation at 1909 N. Clifton Ave., Chicago, and was cited for violations of the Clean Air Act. Source: https://www.epa.gov/il/general-iron.

44 Source: https://abc7chicago.com/general-iron-news-chicago-move/10609679/

45 Source: https://www.chicagotribune.com/news/breaking/ct-scrap-shredder-chicago-permit-southeast-side-general-iron-20220218-tcqs2xvpinadpehvtlkk5zzr3a-story.html.

46 Illinois' eviction moratorium ended in early October 2021. Source: https://abc7chicago.com/eviction-moratorium-illinois-rent-chicago-rental-assistance-end-date/11078484/

I was hired by ASE[47] in June 2020, and they asked, "What do you do [when things are hard enough to want to step away]?" Well, my grandfather did pass away in 2020 at the end of December. He died because of COVID. [He] didn't really love me or appreciate me, so it was really hard. But seeing my father go through a traumatic experience and seeing the rest of my family...it was just... it was difficult. I said, "I need to get some time to make sure my family is OK," because I was always prioritizing the community.

It got hard. I'm not going to sugarcoat it and say it was easy. We got through it. There's moments that are hard, but do we give up? Sometimes it's healthy to walk away, but what example are we setting for youth—that we give up on the community? What does it mean for them?

My parents are immigrants, and [when I was] 16 years old, my parents kind of called out my privilege. They're like, "You're a white Latino, you're male, you have papers, so you have citizen status. You have a voice, right? Nobody can take away that voice. What are you going to speak up for?" It was like a challenge. They're like, "What are you going to do with your life?" Because at that time, I was really smart, but I just hated school, so they were challenging me. What's the point of having everything in a privileged sense, and what do you do with it?

I remember they said, "You should maybe volunteer with Centro de Trabajadores Unidos[48] and maybe see if you like it," so I volunteered to help the fundraising events. I thought it was pretty cool. Then. in college, my friend Kevin's like, "You should start in student government because the way you talk, people listen, but you have to learn to articulate your message."

I always [say] on social media that you start educating people with your family. My parents are very giving people. They've always allowed me to use what I needed, the resources that they provided. They're devout in their religion; they really care about giving back to the community. Conversations [have] been difficult because of the way that they've been brought up, but we understand that other systems are possible. I'm really appreciative of [my] parents being open-minded, us having conversations about gun violence, of race and anti-Blackness in Latin America.

One thing I'll say is—because I'm always organizing, always in the community—it does bring up tensions. I'm known for making video content and creating photos. When my grandfather passed away, and I visited my grandmother, I created a video [about her] and I put it online. I had one of my cousin's comment saying, "You shouldn't post this. Like, you barely visit, and this is the first thing you do after

---

47 Alliance of the Southeast

48 CTU is a workers'-rights organization on Chicago's East Side. Source: https://centrodetrabajadoresunidos.org/

the funeral?" This is three months after my grandfather died. They said, "You shouldn't do this. How dare you?"

And I said, "My way of grieving is different. I've been involved in my community. I'm putting my heart and soul into this, and I'm trying to get a connection with our grandmother. I'm trying to actually be here." We got on a call to talk so then they understood where I was coming from. It's always about being clear in your intention and stop having your ego get in the way of the community. Family is a part of your community. We can't deny that.

. . . .
. . . .
. . . .

In 2018, Luis Cabrales[49] made a post on Facebook addressing that we need to challenge the negative stigma in our community, and I'm hit with a question "What do I do?" The question comes from the feeling that I didn't feel connected as a community member in the Southeast Side. I got involved in southwest communities from college friends that lived there that asked me, "Hey, you know, we like the work you're doing here on campus. You want to come join us in the Southwest Side to organize our folks?" Sure, cool. So I'm in the Southwest Side helping organize over there.

But [Cabrales] made a post saying, "Hey, for the folks leaving our communities [and] talking badly, leaving this negative stigma—look at how you're affecting our youth. You're causing these issues by creating this negative stigma, by creating this negative atmosphere that's saying nothing can grow, but we're going to prove you wrong." I shared the thought with my mother and then she asked me to reflect—why am I [working] in the South*west* Side when I live *here*? What am I doing for my own community? What [does] my community mean to me?

I DM'd[50] him [and we] talked on the phone the next day, [saying], "Hey, we should create an organization for youth. Let's work on it. I have some experience." He's like, "I'm down," and that's how the Southeast Youth Alliance was born. From that point, we've met weekly and said, "How are you amplifying youth?"

[When] we take care of our youth, we take care of our innocence in a sense. A lot of people that are grown are still youth because they have that innocence in them.

I have mantras. One is: "Who do you want to be today?" What do you want to be doing today? Do it. You want to be a catalyst for your community? Want to be a facilitator? You want to be somebody who people look up to? Well, fine. Then come with actual work, so let's promote the actual work and actual involvement in actual love and tender[ness].

---

[49] Cabrales is an organizer with the Chicago Conservation Leadership Corps. Source: https://www.nrdc. org/stories/meet-chicagoan-determined-break-down-barriers-outdoor-inclusion-latino-people-him
[50] Direct messaging, a person-to-person communication available on social-media platforms like Facebook, Twitter, and Instagram.

VIRUS CITY

I take the initiative, but I also take the initiative to invite other people to take over. That's the whole point. Power isn't individual. Power is collective, and power is meant to be distributed.

We had a lot of our folks dying. We [the Southeast Side/10th Ward] have one of the highest cases of asthma, highest cases of cancer, highest cases of respiratory issues in Chicago.[51] Right now, we have some of the highest cases of COVID,[52] and it's really tragic.

Right when things are about to hit the fan, the people who feel it right away are our communities, low-income Black and brown communities because we start seeing certain items not being available in our area. We understand this and we fight against this [because] we're not a priority for the city, because we're low-income Black and brown individuals. You hear the news of this disease coming out and everybody's thinking, "What's going to happen?"

Once things hit the fan at the start of the pandemic, many Southeast Side organizations came together. [I] was with the [ASE] and the Southeast Youth Alliance, but there's a bunch of organizing centers working for peace together. We[53] came together and said, what is going on? And there was a shortage of resources, so first we created a space for us to vent, a space for us to talk. We had organizers crying, saying, "I'm feeling sick. I have respiratory issues. If I die, what happens to my children?"

It was really a traumatic experience. I remember thinking to myself, *How will we survive if it seems like we're losing hope so fast?* Then I remember we said, "Everything's OK. We have each other's backs. Not all of us know each other, but we care for our community and we're going to care for each other. [We're] going to get through this, so what do we need?"

When we're in these meetings, when we had mothers crying, when we had fathers crying... you see all this vulnerability. How do you not break down? You don't internalize it in that moment. You let it fuel you for what you need. You're like, "I need to be what this person needs me to be."

During June [2020], [after] the murder of George Floyd, there was a lot of tension. I had left town that weekend. I called my parents, but they said, "The expressways

51 Source: https://www.cdc.gov/pcd/issues/2020/19_0265.htm
52 Source: https://www.chicago.gov/city/en/sites/covid-19/home/latest-data/2020-05-03.html
53 The Southeast Environmental Task Force, Alliance of the Southeast, and Centro de Trabajadores Unidos

are closed down. You can't get back." I remember getting to my [cousin]'s house and staying up on the phone all night and just organizing people. I didn't get any time to enjoy being with my family. It was me and my cousin, and he was like, "You didn't come here to come hang out. You came here to plan a protest." Yeah. I mean, this is what I do.

We said, we need these resources, and we need to make sure we clean up. We need to make sure that we show up for the place that got looted in our area of South Chicago, and South Chicago is one of the lowest income areas on the Southeast Side. It's almost ten to fifteen thousand less in income [than] the median income [of] the neighboring community.[54] We were on the phone organizing, saying we need to make sure we come out the next day promoting peace and unity, solidarity with the Black Lives Matters movement.

We had over one hundred people come out and just help clean up the streets. And we needed that. But that week was really tense. Every day there was gunfights. Gang members came out looking to, quote-unquote, defend the communities against looters. Then there was gunshots and fires.

Community members from Hegewisch[55] created traffic stops at the entrances to the community. They said, "Unless you tell us where you live, you can't come in." Hegewisch is known for being a really conservative neighborhood. I remember one of my friends said the community members that made the border to do traffic stops at the entrances asked him to join, and he knew it was because he was Mexican, so they wouldn't look racist. I told them, [people are] racist because [they're] racist, not because they look racist.

We needed to make sure we demonstrated solidarity, so we organized this autonomous thing in two days. We had over five hundred people show up, and you could really see people having that tender loving care and that desperate need for alliance during this time in the pandemic.

It was a really frightening experience too, because I kid you not, there were so many cops in riot gear. We felt outmatched, and they would try to tame us.

The week after that, there was another march, another one we did from the East Side, from the Tank[56] all the way to Eggers Grove.[57] And then we just kept doing protest after protest, teach-in after teach-in.

---

[54] Source: 2008-2012 Census Data: https://data.cityofchicago.org/Health-Human-Services/Census-Data-Selected-socioeconomic-indicators-in-C/kn9c-c2s2/data; 2015: http://www.pbchicago.org/uploads/1/3/5/3/13535542/10th_ward_data_sheet.pdf
[55] A neighborhood on the far South Side of Chicago, bordering Indiana. Source: https://www.chicagomag.com/city-life/a-trip-to-hegewisch-chicagos-most-remote-neighborhood/
[56] "The Tank" is the East Side memorial that honors US veterans of the 10th Ward.
[57] Eggers Grove is a Cook County forest preserve site along the Illinois-Indiana border. Source: https://openlands.org/places/eggers-grove-2/

We were the folks doing marches on the weekends, and then we were doing food pantries during the week. It lifted all the youth's spirits because a lot of the youth [are] always shut down, because this is a police-state community. A lot of these community members believe in [having a larger police presence]. They believe in cops. They believe that if you work hard enough, you'll be uplifted, but a lot of times for minority groups, it isn't a glass ceiling. It's a concrete ceiling.

After this happened, we all talked about a local polluter in July [2020]. General Iron is moving in from the North Side from a white, rich neighborhood to a Black and brown community.[58]

We weren't getting enough response from our local alderwoman [Susan Sadlowski Garza] about General Iron, about the permitting. We had all this built-up rage. We were like, "No, this [General Iron's move to the South Side] is environmental racism. You do not let this happen. Your local representatives are not speaking up for us." We[59] marched to [Alderwoman] Garza's house. We held her accountable.[60]

From there, we built this coalition. We said we would need to have a chair at the table, so we put another coalition specifically tackling environmental racism.

. . . .
. . . .
. . . .

My parents were against me going on [the] hunger strike. [But] afterwards, when I visited my grandmother, we talked, and she asked me what I do. She knew about the hunger strike, and [even though] she has dementia, she still remembered. She's telling me in Spanish, "Oh, yeah, I know you're fighting that polluter." I'm like, "Yeah, how'd you know?" She said, "Ah, I remember watching it on TV," and my mom said, "Yeah, I put it on while I took care of her."

My grandma was like, "Do you like what you do?" I'm like, "Yes," and she's like, "Then I'm happy. You keep doing what makes you happy and that makes me happy." That was one of the first times I heard a family member say that.

58 Source: https://blockclubchicago.org/2020/06/25/state-environment-regulators-approve-general-irons-move-to-east-side/
59 The Southeast Youth Alliance, The United Neighbors of Tenth Ward, and Bridges // Puentes.
60 Source: https://rampantmag.com/2020/11/we-are-not-the-citys-garbage-can/

During this hunger strike,[61] I learned how powerful community is. It's how we take care of each other's health. It's learning that just taking a step back, really taking a step back and letting people being uplifted. I really learned to not take [on] too much, learning about meeting people where they are and understanding topics and conversations.

The most important piece I've learned is that we do this work with love, wanting the best for one another [and] wanting to make sure we're taken care of. When we do that, you don't get tired, or you feel constantly restored by letters of encouragement from high school students, from the youth you work with, from your coworkers or friends. You keep going. Together.

— ANNA GERWIG

---

[61] Nine people participated in the thirty-day hunger strike, which ended on March 4, 2021. Source: https://www.theguardian.com/us-news/2021/mar/07/chicago-hunger-strike-against-recycling-plant-ends

I conduct myself in a specific way anyways because I prefer to keep distance between me and other people. I've always been a man of personal space, and now everybody's like me.

When My Eyes Were Opened

CHI NEWSON, MUSICIAN, GROCERY STORE WORKER

Chi Newson is a musician who produces and performs his own music. He worked at a Jewel-Osco grocery store in the Hyde Park neighborhood on Chicago's South Side at the beginning of the COVID-19 pandemic. There, he experienced firsthand the changes and adjustments that came with the pandemic and the Black Lives Matter protests that occurred around Chicago after the death of George Floyd in Minneapolis at the end of May 2020.

Today, Newson lives in the Oakland neighborhood on the South Side. He is a father of three sons, one of whom was born during quarantine. He was unvaccinated at the time of this interview in October 2021.

INITIALLY, I DIDN'T TAKE IT AS SERIOUS when we were getting all the alerts. I was reading mostly everything that was happening in other countries, and I wasn't really looking at the states here. It's funny, the person that I was living with, we were watching [the movie] *Contagion* like days before [COVID-19] became news. This was in the beginning of March, April. That's when it was an eye-opener: This is different. The world is different.

When the pandemic started, I was working in Jewel, and the grocery scene was just completely different. It was a lot more customers, believe it or not. The entire store was just getting empty in seconds before the riots. They were kind of grabbing everything. Everybody was basically trying to get what they can.

I [could buy] everything first with a discount, so I never really had a shortage. I don't know if I'm allowed to say that. It was legal. I'd definitely set things to the side so when I clocked out, I could go get it.

And then all the apps started going crazy, like Instacart and DoorDash. Eventually it got to a point where there were only deliverers coming into the stores instead of the actual customer.

We didn't necessarily know how to react to customers and how to really act as the people who worked there. We had to keep our mask on, we had to wear gloves, sanitize. At first, if your temperature was up, you couldn't come into work.

Wearing a mask took a while for everyone to adjust to. [Employees] didn't take it as serious at first, and eventually our store managers started to enforce these rules in order to go to work. People were respecting and people wasn't respecting it. You could see what [the mask mandate] was doing to different people and how different people reacted to it.

Working, just, like, staying consistent and trying to persevere through this pandemic, was a lot harder because it affected me mentally as well. It did have a mental effect on my career. If you ask me, I don't think working will ever change from here.

I feel like grocery shopping has changed as well. Before, I was able to pick things up and feel comfortable, like vegetables and fruit. Like, "Oh, OK, this is better than the other." But now I'm kind of hesitant to really touch things because you don't know who's touching those fruits. Now I want fruit that's wrapped already. I want packaged fruit, I want packaged vegetables. I want canned things.

The six-feet thing makes a huge difference. I mean, people are just more conscious of it now. I never really had intentions to go to large gatherings or anything like that. I conduct myself in a specific way anyways because I prefer to keep distance between me and other people. I've always been a man of personal space, and now everybody's like me. So, for me, it's beautiful. For a lot of people, [it's] something to adjust to.

· · · · · · · ·
· · · · · · · · · · ·
· · · · · · · · · ·

I'm active. I like to run, go to the gym, and I play basketball. Ever since the pandemic started, I still haven't played basketball, so I've missed out on a lot of activities I would normally do for health reasons.

I don't like to say this, but I am a person who is affected by depression. At the beginning of COVID, the fact that we weren't able to interact with so many people—eventually it does take a toll on you. It doesn't even have to just be [not] having interactions, it can just be from not going outside.

I missed out on a lot of daylight and stuff like that. It put me in a mood, and it made me learn how to find different sources to make myself feel better, like meditation and self-care and stuff. You start to deal with yourself more than others. We're forced within the last two years to do so. It was an eye-opener.

I guess [quarantine] affected me positively just by self-care, paying attention to myself. My health definitely. I was a lot more productive because there was a point where I was at home, and I couldn't just not do anything, so I had to keep myself as active as possible. Things you have to get done at home got done quite quickly.

I moved into an apartment during the pandemic, so I was able to focus on that because I didn't have to have too much contact and interactions as much as I used to. Now everything is open, and I don't even want to go out anymore, so I save a hefty amount of money.

A lot of people wouldn't even, like, look for connection prior to COVID. Now when you have that chance to talk to somebody else, [you do]. We want to connect with others now.

∴∴∴∴∴∴∴
∴∴∴∴∴∴∴∴∴

I've learned a lot more about how to market my music. So, you know, I've been focusing on getting some material out and being able to make money off of it. [The music business] changed a lot—for good and bad—but mostly positive because I can make more money off of it now.

The way I was making money from music was performing. That affected my income because the performing was different. Everyone wanted to try something new and something different, [like] bringing apps out. It was just different for me. I didn't know I could make as much money as I did when I was performing because, if you ask me, I make double the amount in two weeks. Or triple.

I like to have contact with people I perform in front of. So trying to do the song performances and all of these things, it just got a bit harder until I kind of got the gist of how this works: OK, so maybe I need to focus on a different aspect of my music, like recording and publishing and distribution. Like more of the things you can do now on the internet.

∴∴∴∴∴∴
∴∴∴∴∴∴∴

My mother was my number one concern [during the pandemic] because she's a cancer survivor. Her immune system is compromised so I had to take extra precautions. I had to, you know, double that precaution just because of my mother. I couldn't risk having her sick. I didn't want to bring anything to her, so I had to be extremely cautious.

I lost my grandmother due to COVID—well, not even due to COVID, just due to her health. There was a lot of sketchy, scary things happening as far as her body. When she passed, [she] was laid with other COVID patients, and they had to list her as a COVID patient because they already had the body there.

We all know she didn't have COVID because we were there when she was in the hospital before she passed. Family was there. We couldn't even have her there at the funeral just because that happened. It was a mistake. We had to cremate her instead of giving her a proper burial.

It sounds like a conspiracy, honestly. If we really knew, I'm pretty sure we would have money right now. It was just something that was wrongly done. They added her to COVID patients to—in my eyes—add to statistics. They wanted to implant fear so people can follow the COVID guidelines, which are necessary, but that affected my family. It was a lot for me to even just fathom why this was happening to us.

And I had a son. When we went to the hospital, that's when they opened my eyes, how serious it was. We had to go through all of these procedures. They ask you all these questions: "Do you have a slight cough? Do you feel sick? Do you have a fever?" When my two oldest sons were born, they didn't ask those questions.

We were there just two days, but they rushed us out of there. They didn't want us to stay there because it was mainly COVID patients. But it was one of those moments when my eyes was finally opened, and it became a little bit more scarier. The pandemic was happening, and it was just like I said—I didn't understand it.

After my son was born, we had to go to the hospital because you have to go for basically monthly checkups and stuff. So, I've always consistently had to go to the hospital in the beginning, but it was different [this time]. Like how we had to get in there. There was a point where me and the mother couldn't go in at the same time, so we had to take turns.

When you have a child with someone, normally if you're both working together, one person is better at retaining information, one person is better at being more assertive. So we had to split the responsibilities and learn to kind of cover everything. So that's proved how everything is changing, you know? When we finally learned how things would change, we changed.

Now when I go in, I ask a million and one questions I've never asked at the hospital before. I opened my eyes and was like, "Yeah, this is real."

········
::::::::::···
·········

I don't really have much ambition to go out and get the vaccinations. I mean, if I have to I will, and if I don't have to I probably won't. I know I've been healthy. I have not been sick since the beginning of the pandemic.

What will make me feel safe to get [the COVID vaccine] is to hear more stories from the top one percent. Like, just to hear that, OK, they have their vaccines, it's the same exact things that they're giving out to people and having the same type of body response that we all are. That will convince me, just because I am sure almost everything that's happening now are all going to technically be trial runs. I don't want to be just an experiment.

What will make me get it right now will be because I wouldn't be able to do anything. You have to have your vaccination card to go out or to participate in these activities. If that's the only way—especially with me having children and wanting to do things—then yes, I'm going to do that. I will risk it all just to experience things with my children.

—ANNA KLINGMAN

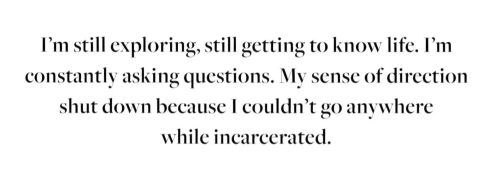

I'm still exploring, still getting to know life. I'm constantly asking questions. My sense of direction shut down because I couldn't go anywhere while incarcerated.

The Big Year

NELSON MORRIS, PRISONER ADVOCATE

Nelson Morris, 46, sat on the couch in his apartment where he lives with his fiancée, Sherry. In the background, his pet parrot made outraged noises, which combined with the clinking of dishes, the microwave, and the oven timer. His fiancée was home. The interview took place on February 1, 2021, which was marked by a heavy snowfall and low temperatures.

Morris was incarcerated at the age of 17 for murder and released in August of 2020. He was resentenced after the Miller decision,[62] which requires re-evaluation in the case of minors convicted for life without parole.

Now Morris works as a prisoner advocate at Restore Justice Illinois, an organization dedicated to providing advocacy and support for incarcerated individuals. He was very open and willing to talk about his experiences both in prison and the outside world, which is now like a foreign land to him.

DO I FEEL SECURE? No, I don't. I don't think so, no. I know I don't.

I was a juvenile lifer. At the age of 17, I was sentenced to natural life and thirty-five years in prison. I did twenty-nine years and a month in jail. Now I work for Restore Justice. I'm the program associate. I've been free for about five months, something like that. Big year for me.

Early in [2020], by February, March, that's when we really started hearing about COVID. I had already been resentenced and everything, so I knew that I was coming home. I was in a minimum [security] facility, so everything was about COVID. And it was known, the fear of it. Trying to get the staff to be more serious about it because they really weren't at the time.

They stopped all our visits in March. I remember this very clearly, because my birthday is March 19, and [the prison] stopped visits, like, March 16, right around my birthday.

---

[62] The US Supreme Court ruled in 2012 in *Miller vs. Alabama* that a sentence of life without parole for a juvenile offender amounts to cruel and unusual punishment. In a second court case, *Montgomery vs. Louisiana* (2016), the court decided that Miller must apply retroactively to young offenders who had previously been sentenced to life without parole. Source: https://www.supremecourt.gov/opinions/11pdf/10-9646g2i8.pdf Source: https://www.supremecourt.gov/opinions/15pdf/14-280_3204.pdf

They still haven't started visits back from what I hear. That's my first time when the prisons were like, "Oh, no more visits." No yards. Shut everything down. So that's how we knew for sure, from the reaction of the prisons.

I didn't get to see no one for my birthday. No one. I was kind of scared because usually, they stop visits and say, "Hey, this is why we stop," and we resume visits later. But no, they said, "No more visits until further notice." And that's really scary. That's when I realized how serious this COVID thing really was.

I was most frightened of the complications of COVID and getting sick. At the time, we heard about all these people dying and how you need to social distance. Well, you can't social distance in prison. You can't clean your surroundings in prison—you know, you have no power over any of that. I just really was scared for my well-being. My health.

I was at minimum [security] at the time, so we shared toilets, we shared sinks. It was a community bathroom. So, everything you did was amongst each other. And they [the media and guards] talked about this disease and how it's contagious. You couldn't risk using the phone because, you know, they were saying this was airborne.

We started to receive masks, like, maybe a few months in, like June. We had masks a few months before I came home. Luckily, the place I work for, Restore Justice, I was in contact with them, and they were keeping up with [the COVID situation]. They were keeping up with the Department of Corrections, like, "Hey, why don't you don't have any masks?" They helped a lot. They got officers to wear the masks and to take it seriously.

[The officers] really didn't take it seriously at first. They thought it was, like, a gimmick or fraud, and they was living their life. The whole entire lockdown they was bringing their own food, and then got a mask and took the mask off. It was real bad before they also started getting sick themselves. It was really bad.

COVID took a while to get there, fortunately for myself, but everybody I kept up with, still keep up with, has had COVID since I left. I've been home for five months and everybody I keep up with has had COVID in the prison. You know that's scary. Everybody was like, "You lucky, son. You left, everybody just start catching COVID." I had one friend pass. Everybody else is pretty much doing OK.

When I was still there, they were taking our temperatures every morning and every evening. I heard now that they make the officers take the test. I made arrangements right before I left, and I made them test me before I was sent home. I put the right grievances in the paperwork. Like, "Hey, you know you're not about to send me home to family, and I might have this disease and you're not going to test me?" You know, so I wrote grievances and grievances,[63] and they tested me before I left.

---

[63] An Inmate Grievance Form is used when the inmate has a question or complaint regarding custody treatment, medical treatment, jail policies and procedures, or other related matters.

My family, they was really nervous for me, but at the same time, I've been gone twenty-nine years and the happiness of me coming home to be home kind of overrode [the nerves].

My fiancée and one of my closest friends—who also was a juvenile lifer; he did twenty-five—they came to pick me up from prison. And it was really odd, because they signed the necessary paperwork, but when I walked out, there was nobody in the lobby. It was like a ghost town. When I got to the front door, [the officers] like, "No, you got to come out the side door," and then another side door. They wouldn't let my fiancée or my friend get out the car. They had to drive up, and then I had to get in the backseat and then drive off. We couldn't get out the car until we were off the grounds.

[The parole board] didn't send me to my planned parole site. My former employer opened up her home to me with her husband and her children. She helped me, because I didn't even know how to use a cellphone. I knew I had to become familiar [with technology] in order to do the job I do. I know that I had to know a lot more than I did back then, so I stayed with her for a few months, just to learn how to work a phone, a laptop, things of that nature.

I'm learning basic life skills. Thirty years is a long time, you know. Like, the phone will ring, and I [won't] accept the call. I did not know how to swipe up, so it will ring, and I'll call you back because I couldn't actually answer the phone. 'Cause I never had a phone before. Just going to the mall or the public bathroom—I didn't know about sensors, so I didn't know how to, you know, wash my hands or flush the toilet.

The biggest culture shock was technology. Like, when I came home, you can't even watch TV without Wi-Fi. You can't just turn the TV on, you need Wi-Fi for your TV and this and that. Oh, and not needing cash. Like, everything is cards now, and there's been places don't accept cash. Things like gas. We get gas and we used the card. That was really weird to me.

I'm still exploring, still getting to know life. I'm constantly asking questions. My sense of direction shut down because I couldn't go anywhere while incarcerated. I went back to my old area where I grew up, and I don't even recognize anything. If it wasn't for GPS, I couldn't get anywhere.

I never had a driver's license, so I had to go get a test. I'd go and take the written test, take the driver's test, the whole thing. And then just [to] buy a car and not having any credit because it's like, "Hey, man, you don't even exist." I had been incarcerated since I was a kid, so I never had a bill in my name. I've never had a job, I've never paid taxes. I have zero credit. So that was a challenge in itself.

At the car dealership, [the salesman] at first was like, "Well, we can do nothing for you."

And then I was like, "Hey, man, look, I've been incarcerated for nearly thirty years. I've been gone since, like, 17."

When I actually explained my situation, he's like, "Look, we can work something out."

People, I noticed, when I tell my story even now, [they] give me ideas. First it was really challenging, but once I told my story, they were like, "No, let me help," and, "We going to make sure you have stuff." Lot of people surprised me. You get good-natured people that really will go out of the way to make sure I got the things I needed once they knew my situation. If it weren't for them good people, things could have been a lot worse, but because of them I was able to get my license, get me a car, open the bank account.

I did expect more reservation from people. You are closed off around the people that you're around, being in jail for so long. You just automatically assume that most people are like those people. So you don't expect to see good come out of most, because even law enforcement [surprised me]. You're just pleasantly surprised that people's better natures are still there.

I was fortunate to have people in my life. My fiancée. Very fortunate, because my employer, she would visit me for years. She never failed me for years. And I started working a week after coming home. Which means I started getting a paycheck two weeks after coming home. That did wonders. It stopped me from having to rely on other people. I was able to pay more bills. Independence is very important to me—not to have to ask anybody for nothing, not to have to go, "Can you lend me this? I need your help." If you show me that I got the resources to do it myself, just show me how. That's where I'm at right now. You don't do it for me. Just show me how.

. . . .
. . . .
. . . .

The early release policy[64] was implemented. I deal with it through my job. It was horrible. I'm not one to use the race card, you know, but I was in a minimum [security] facility, so I was around a lot of guys that had short-time [sentences]. And the guys they let go was all white people. I was talking to my boss [at Restore Justice] about it, like, "Hey, I don't wanna sound crazy or make you feel uncomfortable," because she's white. She started laughing, because she's like, "We just did a report on this, and that's what the numbers said.[65] So, you're not going crazy."

---

[64] Illinois Governor J.B. Pritzker signed an executive order dated March 26, 2020, that was meant to allow medically vulnerable prisoners early release in order to mitigate the spread of COVID-19 in the prison population. Source: https://www2.illinois.gov/Pages/Executive-Orders/ExecutiveOrder2020-13.aspx
[65] The Restore Justice Illinois report, "Illinois Failing Key Pillar of COVID-19 Response," can be found at https://restorejustice.org/early-releases-exacerbate-racial-inequity/.

It is heartbreaking, you know. I've been gone thirty years. I've been in max prisons and all this time managed to stay out the way and out of trouble, and I can't get no good time off [when] the law say I can? You don't want to give it to me, but you're letting all these white dudes go home? It's heartbreaking. It really is, but you get over it. You say, "OK, how can I get home?" I just stayed in school. I did everything I could to better myself while I was incarcerated despite them not wanting me to.

The system is with me on paper. But not really.

I did what I could to better myself. I got my GED[66] in jail, and I did so many different courses. That's how you get good time. Actually, we're looking for grants now and stuff so that maybe I can get into a program. I would want to become a social worker. I think about going [to school], but I'm so tired of classrooms. I really want to do it online if I can.

That's the plan [to go to school], but life happens. It's so much stuff going on now, with the corona. And I'm just being adaptive.

I got grandchildren too. I'm trying to get to know them at the same time I'm trying to adjust to being in a full-blown relationship, and so it's been a lot. And then the everyday work stuff.

I also am a mentor at Precious Blood.[67] It's a Catholic organization. They mentor youth. I do that three times a week, so I go to the city. I meet two kids three times a week.

The kids are really sweet. I've taken a few of them out already. We rented out a movie theater and took, like, twenty kids up to the movies like a couple days ago. It was pretty cool just to see them, how they can open up to you in this way. This is gratifying. This is cool.

My plate be pretty full.

I'm trying [to] do as much life as I can. At the same time, I'm trying to do positive things as well. I grew up in a single parent household, and I got involved with gangs and drugs not because I had to. My mother kept food on the table, worked two jobs. [The gangs] was there, and I fell off into that. If I had a mentor, maybe I wouldn't. That's why I mentor kids three times a week. And my job is so cool, fully paid. They let me do it.

It's amazing, what I have. I came home. The Department of Corrections still want to have so much access, all day every day. What I can do, what I can't do. My parole officer can still pop up anytime. I have to register as a violent offender, so if I move,

[66] General Education Development exam, a high-school equivalency test
[67] Precious Blood Ministry of Reconciliation serves the Chicago neighborhoods of Back-of-the-Yards and Englewood. Source: https://www.pbmr.org/about-us

I gotta notify. If I leave town, I gotta notify them and my parole officer. If I go to any other state, I gotta let them know.

I did get to vote. It was a big deal. I did my research on all the judges. I wanted to vote. I registered when I came home and, finally, was able to get my state ID. So, by the time it came around, I was ready to go. I get my ballot; I did the mail-in ballot because I didn't trust the COVID thing. It was my first time. My first vote. It was really cool. For the rest of my life, I will vote.

Excuse the bird. He's in the cage now, and he is used to flying around. He became loud a little bit when not [out of his cage]. This is the first time I got a pet. This is something, because, you know, it's somebody to take care of, worry over. Like people keep making fun of me and all, like, "Of all these things, you got a bird?"

I don't lock [the parrot] up during the day. I let them roam around and all that. You got to take care of them. Like, he missed flying around. I don't know if you can see him. You know, it what's cool. This is cool to take care of something else.

I'm a dog person, but with being on parole they won't let me have a dog I want. I opted to just let that go. I just got me a bird.

2021 is my first full year being free. That's exciting. My fiancée was just talking about it. We were at the store yesterday, and we finally started digging ourselves out the snow. We was looking for salt. It was just mountains and mountains of snow, and I was just like, "Wow, it's everywhere," and she was like, "Oh, he's never seen it before." And I'm like, "Yeah, I haven't."

My fiancée, Sherry, has helped me do everything. Everything, period. It seems weird, but she has been my friend, my mother, my everything. My mother passed years ago, so [Sherry] had to show me everything. Like, literally, how to pump gas. Car maintenance, house maintenance, how to pay bills. How to open up a bank account.

It's not fair to her. You asked what I want to tell her? "I love you. Even if I don't show that how I should....I love you."

I'll see her trying. It's a challenge, you know, being with me. So, I will say "I love you." To wake up in the middle of the night and she there... I told her, she is everything. To learn a person, just learn how to cohabitate. It's been a learning curve. And then she deals with my shit.

We're waiting to plan a wedding. Is it a COVID decision or a life decision? Both, I think. I really want to marry her now, but she said that I need to grow up a little bit more. When we do, we want family around; we want our kids around. We want it to be a celebration.

We been talking about getting a cabin. I want a cabin in Wisconsin or something like that. We already actively talking about vacations. We were lying in bed yesterday literally talking about vacations we're going to do. I have to get permission from my parole officer, and thank God the parole officer I have now, he seemed really understanding, so I don't think it's gonna be a problem to go.

All this is new. Never been in a full relationship before. Like, living with somebody, accountable for somebody? All that shit new. Like I said, every day is a different challenge. So yeah, you learn every day. Every day is something different.

I don't feel secure 'cause I know tragedies happen, and I know jobs get lost, but I am making steps to try to feel secure. I know I'm fortunate, but I want to make sure that I continue to be financially stable. I'll do whatever it takes to make sure that happening. I was telling my fiancée I'm looking for a second job. Right now, I'm looking for part time, but if I came across a full-time job, that [would] fit.

I have a church base because of the quarantine, but I am a spiritual person. It is something I want to reestablish in my life. I'll just ask— I would just really hope that people wouldn't judge me from my worst action. Judge me for myself, judge me for how I carry myself now. Just judge me for me. I'm not a monster, you know. I was a kid, I made a horrible mistake. I really believe I did my time for it. I do consider myself a good person that did a bad act. Now leave it like that.

—ANNA KUBIK

...she prides herself in educating her fellow nurses on the necessity of critical thinking and nuanced care in the ICU.

Who Saw This Coming?

SHARON HOLLIVAY-WHEELER, CLINICAL NURSE SPECIALIST

On March 11, 2020, the World Health Organization (WHO) declared the COVID-19 virus a global pandemic. Many healthcare workers across the globe have been laid off or have quit their jobs due to pandemic-life obligations or fear for their safety. According to The Hill, *nearly one in five healthcare workers in the United States quit their jobs during the COVID-19 pandemic.[68]*

Working in the COVID-ICU unit for John H. Stroger Jr. Hospital, the public hospital serving Cook County and also the busiest emergency room in Illinois,[69] Sharon Hollivay-Wheeler has been on the front lines of the battle for survival against COVID-19 as significant numbers of her healthcare peers exited their positions.

During this interview in early November 2021, Hollivay-Wheeler asserted her belief in the power of education. As an Advanced Practice Nurse, in the role of Clinical Nurse Specialist, she prides herself in educating her fellow nurses on the necessity of critical thinking and nuanced care in the ICU.

MY MOTHER USED TO TELL ME that I should either be a nurse or a teacher, because I was always taking care of people from a really young age. She told me that if I wanted to be a nurse, I needed to work at a nursing home. So, when I turned 16, I applied to the nursing home. They turned me down, like, eight times.

But the ninth time that I applied, the lady called me and said, "I'm sitting here looking at nine applications from you. Why don't you come in and let's talk about it?" Then she hired me as a nursing assistant. After that, I went and got training as a nursing assistant at the Chicago Medical Institute[70] downtown. From there, I worked my way through nursing school.

When I was younger, I expected to be able to take care of people. I think I always expected to learn the skills to be able to help people to get from A to B. So, as I grew into nursing, I saw that my education is the tool that I administer

---

68 Source: https://thehill.com/policy/healthcare/575209-almost-1-in-5-healthcare-workers-quit-jobs-during-pandemic-poll

69 Source: https://www.npr.org/local/309/2020/03/12/814937832/treating-uninsured-patients-is-wreaking-havoc-on-cook-county-finances

70 Information about the Chicago Medical Institute was not available, but it appears to be closed.

when people come and get help. I have those resources mentally, I would say, to be able to administer care.

Part of administering care is absolutely mental, because not only do you care for the patient, you care for that patient's family. You have to have some kind of skill to deal with people's different emotions. It's not just giving a shot or giving a pill.

I don't believe I thought about it initially; I just wanted to take care of people. But as I've gotten older, after getting my master's [degree] and wanting to teach, I think I can look at it in a different way. I've always practiced that way, or should I say, I kind of grew into practicing that way. Nursing can be pretty exhausting, because it can take all of you.

· · · · · · ·
· · · · · · · · · · · ·
· · · · · · · · · · ·

Pre-pandemic, I would go to work, and I would just have my regular scrubs on. I still wear my regular scrubs, but you'd be able to just walk on to the unit without worrying about the whole unit being on isolation.

Initial assessment is extremely important because our patients can change within five minutes. The minute you get there, you got a history, and you got a full assessment. There would be certain people who were identified as being on isolation, and there would be a card in front of their door stating that. And you were prepared before you went into the room.

You have to review the patient's history and determine what procedures or plans they would have that day. I go through and look at the test results, and I always read the doctor's plan of care to see which direction we were going in.

My basic principle for my patients is airway breathing circulation. So, first off, are they breathing? Do they have a clear airway? Most of our patients are on a ventilator or have breathing issues; we have to make sure that they're getting the set volumes and set rate[71] that they're supposed to get—the set oxygen. I listen to the lungs and make sure their airway isn't blocked. If it is, I'd have to suction. Behind the tongue accumulates a lot of mucus, so you'd have to make sure you suction back there. Sometimes you may come across a person who's not intubated, and they sound really hoarse, so you've really got to inspect their airway. They may need to be suctioned.

Once you get past the breathing, then it's circulation, cardiac. Is their rhythm normal? Is it a fast rhythm? Am I giving medication according to the rhythm? For cardiac, you have to check pulses, all the pulses that you can feel. And you always want to check urine flow. Do they have a Foley?[72] Are they peeing? When did they

---

[71] The respiratory rate for delivery breaths per minute on a ventilator. Source: https://www.ncbi.nlm.nih.gov/books/NBK441856/

[72] A type of catheter. Source: https://medlineplus.gov/ency/article/003981.htm

pee last? Circulation also includes gastric: are they getting enough feeding? Do they have a tube feeding? Did they have a bowel movement?

Then, you also have to look at skin: skin tone, skin turgor,[73] and touching. The skin is also an organ, so you have to make sure no tubes are pressing on the skin. If a patient can speak, I interview them about how they're feeling and specifically ask them, is this going on or is that going on?

Then I make sure to see what's ordered. For some medications, let's say if the doctor ordered them potassium, I've checked the labs already. I might say, "You know that this patient's potassium is such and such. Are you sure you want to give it to them?"

Sometimes our doctors are very new, and they need a little bit of guidance. They may just impulsively order stuff, but it's up to us at the bedside to be an advocate for that patient. We inform the doctors that this patient has this and that going on, or that this [treatment] may not be appropriate. Or, "Doc, do you think the patient would benefit from this test or from this medication?"

All of this comes together in an assessment on a note. All through the day, you document from there. We are very dependent on blood pressures, heart rate, oxygen saturation; we're monitoring all of that. And we document every hour.

Usually, when I go in, it's like I'm doing all this stuff at the same time, but I'm also making sure the patient is comfortable. Most patients can't move; they're sick and don't feel good, so I make sure that their bed is comfortable for them, repositioning them with care.

Going into COVID, you can imagine it's much worse. It was scary. We actually had a lot of people quit. A lot of nurses retired immediately when they found out it was coming. Before the pandemic was announced, [the Cook County Health Department] started telling us that there was this bad virus coming, and we're going to have to treat it like we treated Ebola.[74] Nurses did not want to take care of those patients the same way they didn't want to take care of COVID patients.

Staffing was horrible because people didn't—and don't—want to work. We had so many call-offs, and we lost so many nurses. I'm in the union, and they complain that the hospital should have seen this coming, but who saw this coming? Who saw a pandemic coming and nurses just leaving? And quitting? Nobody saw that.

VIRUS CITY

---

73 Skin elasticity, a way to check for dehydration. Source: https://www.healthline.com/health/skin-turgor
74 The 2014–2016 Ebola outbreak in West Africa caused more than 11,000 deaths worldwide. Eleven cases were confirmed in the United States. Source: https://www.cdc.gov/vhf/ebola/history/2014-2016-outbreak/index.html

Before you go into the room, you have to put on an N95 and a mask that covers the N95. I like to wear head coverings, so everybody started wearing head coverings too. People also started putting on two or three gowns and double gloves.

Heading into COVID, the hospital administration offered most of the nurses the chance to wear scrubs, so this hit the surgical department hard. Most of the nurses were very afraid. They didn't want to take anything home, so the majority of the nurses started wearing surgical gowns. And the administration was like, "We're running out of surgical gowns. We really need to offer these nurses scrubs."

You have to get all this stuff on while you got a patient in the room who's having trouble breathing, so I found that to be extremely stressful.

Let me just say, for me, that's when my assessment skills came in, because it's important to do a great assessment. If you get a handoff and that patient has been having trouble all night, you can't wait to go in there. You got to go and check that patient out right away, because when our patients get into trouble, they can go downhill really fast.

It all comes with establishing that baseline, making sure you know what's going on with your patient and what kind of trouble they can get into. You need to know where they are. We have to pay attention to body systems and what's going on with that patient.

All of a sudden, our unit turned into a COVID unit, which I knew was going to happen anyway. But staff would refuse to work on the COVID unit. We have two eleven-bed units, "MICU-A" and "MICU-B,"[75] and we would rotate every thirty days. So we would spend thirty days on the COVID side.

It was very stressful. You have staff who are sort of controlling, so we had some charge nurses who decided, "OK, you're going to take care of this patient all the time." And that's really stressful and unfair. So when the pandemic started, you can imagine they didn't want to assign themselves to COVID patients, and the nurses who floated into our unit didn't want to take care of COVID patients either. Everybody was afraid to go into COVID patients' rooms.

At first, if a patient coded, we didn't know what to do. Now it's starting to ease up, but with the [Delta] strain, it's picked back up again. We had COVID patients down to just one side [of the MICU], and then they started filling up the other side again.

Currently, we have potential COVID patients who come and are called a "patient under investigation." Which means that patient has been around somebody who's caught COVID and they're experiencing symptoms, but they haven't tested positive for COVID yet. So, they have to come to the COVID unit.

---

[75] Medical Intensive Care Unit

If they rule it negative, then we hurry up and get them to a place where they are with other negative patients. For us, since we have mostly COVID patients, the other ICUs have had to bear the burden of our negative COVID patients, which I think was a really smart decision, even though the other units don't like it. That's the surgical ICU, neuro ICU, cardiac ICU, and burn ICU. They would take our patients who didn't have COVID, and they hated it. They still hate it. They're like, "We don't want them ICU patients," because our patients are pretty intense. We take care of all the systems: cardiac, neuro, and surgical, so we're normally the dumping ground.

∷∷∷∷∷∷••
•∷∷∷∷•••

A couple of months ago, I got a patient who refused to get the vaccine. She said she'd just come back from a trip to Las Vegas, and when she got on the plane coming back, she started feeling really short of breath. She thought that maybe it was just the altitude. But when she got home, she developed a cough and was extremely fatigued. When she got worse, she came to the hospital, and she tested positive for COVID. Her entire family tested positive as well. She ended up on a ventilator, with a tracheostomy.

I felt so bad for her because she told me she hadn't gotten vaccinated, and her kids weren't vaccinated either. She was so scared that she was going to die. I told her, "We're going to do the best we can for you, so let's take it step by step." I think the hardest part was that her family wasn't allowed to come see her; the doctors could only do video chats with the family. Eventually, she got over it; she did well. She's a success story.

I remember her asking me, "Do you think I can go ahead and get the vaccine now?" Before she left, I do believe she got the vaccine.

∷∷∷∷∷∷
•∷∷∷∷•••

Through learning, we've been able to treat our COVID patients better. Now we see a lot of people getting better. I think that there's a population of people who are more cautious, but there's still a big population of people who don't want to get the vaccine. The patients we've had come in that didn't get the vaccine prior, and they come in so sick, by the time they leave, they're speaking for the vaccine. And, when this new strand [Delta] first started, a lot of people passed away, a lot of unvaccinated patients. Vaccinated patients' symptoms were not as bad, and they did, I would say, quite well.

COVID is highly contagious, and some people show no symptoms. That's the problem. Then they spread it to somebody who's very sick, like Colin Powell.[76] He just passed away from COVID, and they said it was because his immune system

[76] The former chairman of the Joint Chiefs of Staff and secretary of state under George W. Bush died in October 2021 of COVID-19. Source: https://www.nytimes.com/2021/10/18/us/politics/colin-powell-dead.html

was suppressed. So you don't know if you may have caught it, are carrying it and passing it on to others, to somebody who can die from it.

That being said, it's OK if you don't want to get vaccinated. I think we still have a moral obligation to wear a mask, wash our hands, and prevent it from being spread. It's just similar to the HIV virus. If you know you have HIV, you don't go and have sex with everybody; you're cautious to prevent spreading the virus. With COVID, like HIV, you don't always know if you have it, but there are proven ways to prevent the spread. It cannot be taken lightly.

I think that's where thorough education is going to have to be applied. We all have self-preservation instincts, but there are few of us who really care about mankind. So we have to help exemplify that you can't have behavior that's going to put others in danger.

We have a long way to go until we're all at least somewhere on the same page, for sure. Even if we're not on the same page, we should get to a point where we're at least thinking about each other.

—CAMRYN BEACO

How We Want to Grow

MEGAN MORRISON, MARKETING AND COMMUNICATIONS COORDINATOR

Megan Morrison is the marketing and communications coordinator with Growing Home, an urban farm and workforce development center serving Chicago's Englewood neighborhood and dedicated to breaking down employment barriers while providing people with access to healthy food. Morrison previously taught high school arts and English in Boston and volunteered in a garden-club program with elementary schools. She moved to Chicago looking to work with food accessibility and found in Growing Home a program that combined that interest with her background in education.

During this interview in November of 2021, she spoke quickly, finding new layers to explore beneath each subject, like the hidden roots that nourish a plant's bloom.

WE TEND TO USE the [term] "food insecurity" more than "food desert" at Growing Home. Like, there are grocery stores. There's a Whole Foods. But do people have transportation to the grocery store? Are the prices affordable? Are there enough fresh-food areas? And with COVID, the lack of a supply chain in terms of food and grocery stores and everything like that was even [worse]. "Food desert" doesn't describe the whole system of problems.

It's been a whirlwind, obviously, over two years: we didn't have the farm stand, we avoided being inside together. That's where we're at right now. Unemployment rates were already high in Greater Englewood compared to Chicago due to disinvestment, historic segregation. And then it was even higher with COVID.

· · · · · · · · ·
· · · · · · · · · · · ·
· · · · · · · · · ·

[Growing Home is] a nonprofit social enterprise and a USDA-certified organic farm, actually the first and only one in the Chicago city limits. We use our urban farm as a vehicle for nutritious food access as well as workforce development. Our production assistants (PAs) are our trainees in our twelve-week paid employment training program. They come to Growing Home to be a part of our transitional employment program. PAs often have one or

VIRUS CITY

more barriers to employment that they're working through, and Growing Home has wraparound support services to assist them in getting rid of those barriers. We teach people and we pay people at the same time.

[On] a typical day—take a Thursday, like today—our production assistants arrive at 8:30. We can have up to four cohorts a year and up to twenty, twenty-five people in a cohort. So on a Thursday, where maybe we'd have our large group instead of smaller groups, we'd have twenty of our production assistants arrive.

They meet with the farm team at 8:30 a.m. on our farms and start with a morning circle, where we go around and share on a scale of one through ten how we're TIP-ing. It's a term that Growing Home uses based on one of our courses called "Transforming Impossible into Possible." So, "How are you TIP-ing?" Kind of getting a sense of where everybody's at that morning.

Then a little bit of stretching, and then into the field for the morning part of the employment training program: on-the-farm training, learning all the ins-and-outs from seed to sale, planting, maintaining, harvesting, processing, inventory, quality control. Then there's all the soft skills: communication, working together. A typical day. Not back to normal, but back to a little bit how we did before.

I started in July 2020—I've been here for a year and a half—so I'm starting to see what it was like before. It's neat to see, especially with farm stands.

We didn't go to farm stands at all in 2020. We didn't want to put our staff or our production assistants at risk.

On a beautiful day, we have the tents out, we have water, we have cooking demos. We have music playing. We've had times where one of our senior neighbors—she comes every week to help out, volunteer—she takes dancing lessons. She knows how to dance well. She just starts dancing with somebody else who's there. And sometimes other songs come on, and the staff starts dancing with some of the people who are joining in. So that's definitely kind of a weekly grounding touch point I love, and I know a lot of other people do. We really strive to create a space that's welcoming and fun to hang out.

We have the cooking demos, and we have our staff who are alumni of the program or who live in Englewood. Our community engagement coordinator is also an alumni who grew up in Englewood. She does most of the cooking demos. With these connections, we know what our community likes in terms of food. We make sure we grow 80 percent of what our neighbors might want, and then we grow 20 percent of something that might be new. I think that's always a fun part of going to a produce stand, a local farm. Sometimes you would pick up something you haven't tried before.

[Throughout the pandemic] we've been able to be creative and still serve our community. In 2020, we switched to mostly a CSA (community-supported agriculture) model. In this model, a customer pays for an eight-week box subscription that they'll get spread out every other week throughout the season.

We had about twenty CSAs in 2018, and we had about eighty in 2020 because we switched to at-home, contactless deliveries. We didn't do our farm stand. We did wholesale with a couple of organizations like Catholic Charities that are wanting to get fresh produce out to their community. We didn't have the kind of farm stand/ neighborhood kind of community gathering spot, but we still were able to share nutritious, fresh food with everybody.

In 2019 and 2020, we also really focused on looking at how much of our produce was being distributed in Greater Englewood versus going outside to Green City Market or Logan Square Market, which we did previously, but we don't do anymore.

Our new executive director, Janelle, was very focused on [making] sure more than 50 percent of our fresh produce is being distributed in the Growing Home community, in the Greater Englewood community. This year, 2021, we've been able to do 61 percent, and that's not even the full year. And we're continuing to think about how to grow that.

A couple of projects that we're excited about: we don't have plans yet, but we would love to have a Growing Home food truck or food buggy. That's a little different than farming, but it really would allow us to take the cooking demos on the road. And then we could also make it mobile—going back to that piece—if somebody doesn't have transportation to Growing Home, to our farm stand, we could be even more accessible in that way. So that's one project.

The other one, which is kind of a further-down-the-line project that we have: we essentially have four sites at Growing Home, and one is an undeveloped area. It was a concrete parking lot. This year we turned part of it into an experimental community garden. We put down mulch and woodchips, put down some wooden garden beds and raised beds. We have tires—there was somebody who randomly dropped off, like, twenty tires near Growing Home, who knows why. Instead of saying, "Oh, where's somewhere to throw it away," we were like, "Oh, why don't we put some fabric underneath and we'll put soil in, and then we'll grow, like, wildflowers."

One of our ideas down the line is to build a larger community resource center that would house classroom space for our employment training program. But we could open it up to more space for public workshops around employment training, or maybe it's around cooking demos, or preserving and canning. Growing Home becomes a campus hub of community resources.

That's where we're at right now, focused on improving the food insecurity in our neighborhoods, to invest back into the Englewood community.

I'm so grateful to have found Growing Home. I'm learning things every day. Things have been challenging. We're just having to think creatively and figure it out, one month at a time-ish. We're thinking about how we want to grow.

—TOM SHERIDAN

Pandemic Life:
Stories of Resilience

THE FOLLOWING IMAGES were taken by DePaul photojournalism students in 2020. Due to the pandemic lockdowns, students turned their lenses on themselves and their own families for assignments. Their work resulted in a rich photo-documentation of this important moment in history.

At the beginning of the pandemic, I was running around like a chicken with its head cut off. I started picking up shifts at a Macy's fulfillment center. I worked five days a week, six to eight hours a day. I just wanted to stay busy. I didn't want to be home all the time. Being home made me feel stuck.

I was living with my brother and his girlfriend, their son, and sometimes her other kids. We moved during the pandemic from an apartment to a house in Auburn Gresham so we could have more space. It was nice to have a backyard, see the trees, and have a garage. It gave me a sense of privacy and security. It was nice to have flowers and see the sky. There's a freedom, just to be outside.

Self-Healing During the Pandemic

BY JANE ANDREWS

Yoga and meditation have always been really important to me, and the whole idea of self-care. I had to figure out a way to have some me time. For me, dancing is a way to relieve the stress and just uplift yourself. I really like Reggaetón, but I listen to every-thing. Dancing is a form of healing. You're in the moment and in tune with your body.

I'd take care of my nephew in the evenings when his mom went to work. She worked as a CTA bus driver and my brother worked as a forklift operator. They both worked nights sometimes, so I would watch him and put him to bed.

Other times my brother would be home with him during the day. My brother is a playful dad, but also kind of stern. It was crazy with all of our schedules, but we all wanted to make sure that the baby was taken care of.

It was just a lot, dealing with school and having to go to bed early so I could get up at like 4:30 in the morning to go to work. I walked a few blocks to the bus, and took that to the Red Line up to Lake Street. Then I'd come home, knock out some schoolwork and take a nap. Looking back on it, I think, "Wow, Jane. That was a lot." I feel like the pandemic exposed ourselves and how we think. I take everything with a grain of salt. You just have to keep going. Yes, there are obstacles, but it's all in how you approach it.

The beginning of COVID-19 was a very destabilizing experience. But it always made me feel better to get out of bed, put on some makeup, and put on clothes that aren't pajamas.

I lived in Lakeview with two roommates. I didn't go anywhere, so I demarcated time through the things that I wore. I would have a morning work-time outfit, then go to class and change my shirt. Once I put on pajamas, I didn't do work anymore. On the first day of "Zoom university," my roommate and I dressed up and took a photo, just to mark the occasion.

Finding Beauty In New Places

BY AMY DO

I started working out as a coping mechanism. I was doing a lot of Pilates and yoga. I didn't think you could overdo it, but you could. It got to the point where it got to be kind of toxic, and I got tendonitis from overexertion. I was on crutches for a month.

I always find that familiar flavors, smells, and even the rhythms of Japanese and Vietnamese cooking to be very comforting, because that's what I grew up eating. For the first few months of the pandemic, I would make dinner for my roommates every night. It took up some time, and I'd put on an apron. It made me feel like I accomplished something, to put a meal on the table.

Food was such a big part of my quarantine experience. I realized how beautiful it is. If you're looking at a single grape, there are like, fifty shades of purple if you look at it long enough. I looked at this grape for a good five minutes–completely sober—and was like, "Whoa! Look at all this purple!" I learned to recognize the simple beauty in a lot of different things.

Eventually, my roommates were like, "Hey, I want to learn how to make those things." And then eventually they started introducing their own foods. We did the Jewish high holidays together. That was my first experience celebrating a Jewish food tradition, with my roommate's extended family on Zoom. I'm grateful that I got to experience that.

It was a really weird time to be Asian in America. With the anti-Asian sentiment, that sense of, "Oh, it could be me" hits a lot harder. I wasn't heckled, but I definitely know people who were. It was very scary to know that somewhere out there, people didn't believe that I should be alive. I never really talked about it. I just did my yoga, and cooked dinner, and tried to feel OK. I think every Asian has had some kind of complex about their eyes at some point. I didn't realize until later where that came from: media.

One day during the pandemic, I sat down and unfollowed every Instagram account that made me feel bad about myself. I started to curate my social media feeds to be more inclusive and celebratory of Asian excellence. It gave me a more well-rounded sense of what it means to be pretty and healthy.

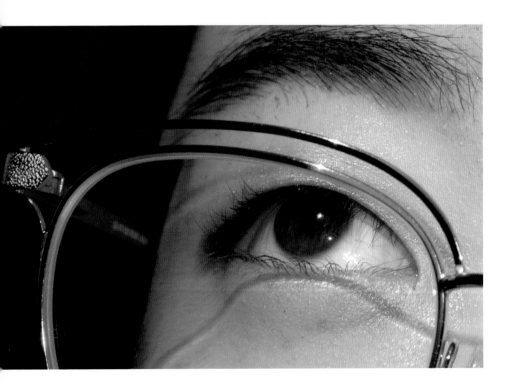

I spent a lot of time looking out our front window. Anytime there was some kind of change, it was very exciting. This one day, after a big rain, this huge puddle appeared. We called it "the big lake." These kids were having a ball getting so wet and disgusting in this gross puddle, but they were having so much fun. It really put a smile on my face. It reminded me that maybe not everything is awful if children can still have fun in big puddles.

Documenting Uncertainty

BY MARÍA MARTA GUZMÁN

I reported live from the protests in Kenosha for the Canadian Broadcasting Corporation (CBC). My immigration story is the reason I went into journalism. My family and I immigrated from Nicaragua when I was 6. There were a lot of challenges: financial, culture shock, the language barrier, living with ten people in a house at times. We would turn on the 5 p.m. news with Jorge Ramos and María Elena Salinas reporting on Univision for the Latino community. I saw myself in them and the stories they reported. I always knew I wanted to be that person for someone else. (Photo by Jonathan Aguilar)

When the pandemic hit, I flew to Miami to be with my family. I just didn't want to be alone. There were only five people on the plane. People weren't wearing masks yet, but I did because my mom told me to.

My mom was a lawyer in Nicaragua. Now she works as a beauty consultant for Tom Ford at Saks Fifth Avenue. She couldn't work during COVID, so there were a lot of financial concerns. I eventually went back to Chicago so I could work to pay my rent. Before I went back, my mom sewed some extra layers onto my masks so I'd be safer.

When George Floyd was murdered, I couldn't watch the whole video. It was just the inhumanity of it. This person was murdered in plain sight. When the protests started, I went to Little Village because I wanted to document the Latino perspective on what was happening.

There was a lot of unity between Latinos and the Black community, and a lot of passion. I think it's because they saw part of themselves and their families in George Floyd. My brother and my stepdad have darker skin than me. It could have easily been them.

The protest was peaceful at first. But as it got closer to downtown, it got more intense. There was so much tension between police and protesters, especially by Trump Tower. People were really angry, and they were reacting to what had happened. It wasn't just about George Floyd. It was Ahmaud Arbery, Breonna Taylor, and so many others. George Floyd was just the tipping point. I do think the protests did have an impact by bringing these issues to our national attention. As an immigrant, I'm thankful to be in this country, but that doesn't mean we should overlook its faults. There's still a lot of work to be done.

This picture means everything. I graduated with a master's degree in communication during a pandemic. When times were hard, I didn't even think I was going to be able to finish my undergrad degree because my family could not afford to send me to school. God always made a way for me. Like Maya Angelou said, "Still I rise." That's literally how I feel. I thank God for blessing me through all of this. (Photo by Gabrielle Bersamin)

Still I Rise

BY LA'INDIA COOPER

*I was born and raised in Englewood. I love my community.
People look out for each other. Even the gangbangers, they'll tell
you, "Go back in the house. It's about to go down." I'm not
making it seem like it's all rainbows, but this is my comfort zone.
The block is changing, though. There are two abandoned
buildings next to my house. One on each side. I don't like living
next door to them. The empty homes bring the community down
and give access to people who are on drugs or homeless. I wish
they would be torn down. If this were a different community,
this would not be happening.*

I live with my Pa-Pa and my grandma. During COVID, Grandma was feeling pretty discouraged because she didn't feel safe to go to the nail shop. So we gave her new PJs and a spa day at home.

I grew up in the church. My grandma taught me to have faith, because if you don't, you live in darkness. So even though we couldn't go to church, we still did communion at home with juice and crackers.

My grandparents have lived here for forty-nine years. They are pillars of the community. Our house is the one that everyone goes to. It's like a safe haven, where all the barbecues and family get-togethers are. My grandma was especially sad about having to isolate, but she took social distancing very seriously. People would stop by out front, or we would host virtual girls' nights and scavenger hunts. It wasn't normal, but we tried our best.

Honestly, the playground closing was one of the saddest days of the pandemic. Murray Park is where kids can go and guys just play basketball— no drama. I used to pass it to go to church and to work. It was a place you'd usually see laughter and life.

My neighbors' kids were doing school at home. Their mom kept them on a schedule, so they went out for "recess" every day. Their mom was trying to make it normal. But it was not normal.

My family would go outside to do double Dutch in front of our house. Normally, we'd be at a mall or a restaurant.

When George Floyd was killed, tensions were already so aggravated because of the shutdown. I think people were just angry and tired. And they felt like they needed to risk their health and safety to go out and protest.

It's unfair to lump together the protesters and the looters. But, I think that's what some people wanted, to say, "They don't deserve to be treated as equal because they act like animals." Some people are just ignorant. John's is a store right around the corner from my house. And they burnt it down. It had been there since I was a child. It was so sad.

My family runs a food truck in front of our house. That summer, they started giving out food. They did it to show people, we're still here. We still support you.

Our friends and family came, but so did other people in the neighborhood. Simply talking to people and seeing people smile, especially kids who came by without parents who said they were hungry. It felt great to serve people who truly needed it.

My sister and I used to fight a lot when we were younger. COVID helped us have more of a friendship than being just sisters. I'm much closer to her now.

My sister made masks at the beginning of the pandemic, just for something to do.

My family talked about what we would do if one of us got sick. Then my grandfather died, not of COVID. After the funeral, everyone in my family got COVID except for me. My mom had it the worst, but she wasn't down for long. Once we were all home together all the time, we all got very frustrated with each other. It's an experience I didn't want to have to go through, but it definitely made me stronger.

I live in Villa Park with my family. I've lived with my family my whole life. We are pretty close-knit, so it helped me not feel so alone when we were on lockdown.

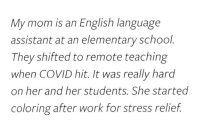

My mom is an English language assistant at an elementary school. They shifted to remote teaching when COVID hit. It was really hard on her and her students. She started coloring after work for stress relief.

My dad works in a freight yard. He kept working through the pandemic. Luckily he didn't have to interact with too many people, but we were still worried.

City on Fire

BY JONATHAN AGUILAR

When the pandemic hit, I was finishing my senior year. I went from doing as much as possible to doing as little as possible. As a photographer, I felt stuck. Shooting with a drone helped me to capture the emptiness, like this mall parking lot. I was like, "OK, this is real. People are taking this really seriously." It's frustrating that in some cities people did so much to protect each other, but not in other places. People aren't taking precautions anymore. I think people just are OK with the amount of people dying, and that's sad.

When the George Floyd video came out, people were marching and protesting. I was like, "I have to get out there and capture this moment in history." I told my family, "I have to do this." They understood me taking that risk. I was so tired of seeing people of color killed in the street. As a person of color, it's something I think about for my family and my cousins, worrying about what could happen. It definitely scares me sometimes.

It felt like a second civil rights movement. Like we were finally going to have a conversation about the police because people were tired and angry and just so upset. I wanted to show that people were willing to take a risk by going out in the pandemic because they stood for something. Looking back on it, I don't think much changed. People were heard, but they weren't listened to.

It was a scary experience. I was like, "Is this really happening? What is this going to devolve into?" I was worried because I heard dogs, and I was like, "Oh my God, they're just going to release dogs on us." That was my biggest fear. I don't think we were ever worried about the protesters. It was always about the police.

A majority of the protests that summer were peaceful, but this one wasn't. It was people's frustrations coming to the forefront. People were fed up and angry and willing to destroy things to share that anger. I don't think this photo is sensational. It just shows what happened.

Some violence broke out between Black and Latinx groups in Cicero. Two people got shot. Right after, there was a Black and Brown Unity Rally, kind of like a response. People didn't want to just focus on the negatives. I mean, both of these groups have experienced so much violence. I think they wanted to show that there's a lot more happening in these communities. There was food and dancing. It was just a huge celebration. I think it was really important to do. The only way real change will happen is to unite the groups who are facing the same issues.

When Jacob Blake was shot in Kenosha, I felt like I needed to be there. One day, I noticed one of the officers had something on her baton, so I zoomed in on it. Later, I realized it was the Miranda rights. I honestly don't know how these issues will be solved if that's what police officers are doing. I photographed several days, but not the one where Kyle Rittenhouse shot and killed two people. Once civilians were willing to kill one another, I knew people would stop protesting because they were afraid. And that's kind of what happened.

A Lot of Commitment

SHEILA MORRIS, ELEMENTARY SCHOOL PRINCIPAL

Sheila Morris, 57, is the principal of Owen Scholastic Academy, an elementary school located in Chicago's Ashburn neighborhood on the South Side. The fall of 2021 marked her fifth year as principal, though she has been in education for over thirty years.

After graduating from DePaul University in 1987, Morris taught at several South Side Chicago schools, such as Mars Hill Elementary in the South Austin neighborhood, Emmanuel Christian School in the Auburn Gresham neighborhood, and Caldwell Elementary School in Avalon Park. Encouraged by her husband, she began teaching at Owen in 2002. From 2008 to 2017, she was the assistant principal, and then she was promoted to principal. However, nothing could have prepared her for 2020. Morris described the chaos of teachers absent for days and printing hundreds of learning packets. Though she faced personal and professional struggles, her faith in God and her loving family kept motivating her.

During our interview, Morris wore her hair in a braided bob. When using hand gestures, she revealed her bright red nails. She spoke in a friendly yet firm voice.

I LOVE CHILDREN. I love seeing when a lightbulb comes on and they understand a concept. I love seeing them excited about trying new things. I love the staff. I love the parents. In my first master's program, I did a thesis on parental involvement. If you have strong parental involvement, you can win the battle of making sure that students are educated. Without that parental involvement and partnership, it is a very hard task.

I love to make people happy, and I love to see collaboration occurring. I just want unity. Sometimes, parents and teachers or parents and administration aren't happy with one another. I have tried, all of these thirty-three years that I've been in education, to make a difference. I want to make a difference at the end of my life. If I have one student that says, "Mrs. Morris made a difference," I will have a heart of happiness.

I was born in 1964 in the Cabrini-Green projects[77] on the North Side. At that time, the projects were a wonderful place to live. I'm number five of six children. My mom and dad were just loving, caring, and hardworking. My mom worked at an airport and a glass company. But then she worked at an elementary school, and she worked in the lunchroom. She had a lot of friends that were teachers, and she would bring me record books. I always, always wanted to be a teacher, so I would play school. All my friends had to be the students, and they got tired of me playing school. They said, "You know what? We're not playing with you no more. All you want to do is play school and be the teacher." I would take attendance and I would try to give them assignments to do.

I went to Friedrich Von Schiller Elementary School.[78] One of my favorite teachers in the whole world was Mrs. McDonald. She was my first-grade teacher. She had a very small frame but a lot of love for the students. She took a liking to me and thought that I was so smart. I liked how caring she was to not only me, but to all of the students. I said, "I want to do that. I want to help students. I want to help people be better." I wish I knew how she was doing now.

After years of being in Cabrini-Green, things started to get pretty bad and violent. It just wasn't safe. My family and I eventually moved out of the projects when I was in sixth grade, which was in 1976. We moved to the South Side of Chicago. My dad was able to get us a house. Oh, my goodness, I was so happy. I used to pray, and I prayed so hard that we could move out.

I graduated from Hyde Park[79] in 1982. I went to Southern University in Baton Rouge, Louisiana, for my first year. My dad is from Louisiana, and most of his siblings went to Southern. I told you I always wanted to be a teacher, but I also always wanted to please my parents. I knew how hard they worked. I would say, "When I become successful and when I do well, I'm going to take care of my mom and dad."

When I was going away to Southern, my mother gave me a $100 bill, you know, to have some money because I'm going thousands of miles away. My dad drove me to school. I had that money in my little back pocket, and somebody pickpocketed me. I didn't have the heart to tell her. That was my mother's last hundred dollars.

[77] Cabrini-Green is a public housing project on Chicago's North Side built during World War II. Source: http://www.encyclopedia.chicagohistory.org/pages/199.html

[78] A public school serving the Cabrini-Green housing projects, Schiller Elementary closed in 2009 by merging with Jenner Elementary. The former Schiller building on W. Scott Street is now the home to Skinner North Classical School. Source: https://web.archive.org/web/20160501203519/http://catalyst-chicago.org/2015/09/can-jenners-terrific-facility-and-strong-arts-programs-overcome-its-history/

[79] A public high school in Chicago's Woodlawn neighborhood on the South Side. Notable alumni include poet Gwendolyn Brooks and aviation pioneer Amelia Earhart. Source: https://hydeparkcps.org/apps/pages/index.jsp?uREC_ID=1604564&type=d&pREC_ID=1733143

I didn't have the money to pay for my books. I was very sad, and I ended up getting a work study job. I overworked myself, and I ended up getting sick. I had gotten the flu. When I came home for Christmas break, I had to be hospitalized. My mom and dad said, "No, you're not going that far away from us anymore." But I was determined. I started searching for some schools in Chicago.

Guess what school I found? DePaul University. My dad kept telling me, "I know you want to be a teacher, but I can see you as a reporter like Oprah Winfrey. You are so good at talking with people." I majored in communications. That is *not* what I wanted to do, but I wanted to make my dad happy.

When I graduated in 1987 from DePaul, I looked *everywhere* for jobs as a reporter. I wasn't getting anything. My brother's girlfriend knew that I wanted to be a teacher, and she told me that her church's school needed a first-grade teacher. The school was on the West Side of Chicago, near Oak Park. I applied, and that's how I became a teacher at Mars Hill Elementary.

For my first teaching job, I want to tell you how much I made. Before I applied, I worked as a computer analyst for American Express. This job paid me $16,000 a year. I thought, "Wow, that's some money." It really wasn't. At Mars Hill, I made $11,000 a year. You would've thought that I was making a million bucks. I was so *happy*. I was decorating my classroom—not paying attention—[and] I accidently stapled my finger. I was in so much pain, but I was still happy.

After a year passed, the school wanted me to do so much. I taught language arts and math to my first-grade students. I also taught second- through sixth-grade students African American studies. Then they had me teaching basic Spanish to second- through sixth-grade students. My husband encouraged me to leave. He said, "Sheila, that's just not good."

I found another Christian school called Emmanuel Christian. They had an opening for a second-grade position. I went from making $11,000 at Mars Hill to $17,000 at Emmanuel. I learned a lot from wonderful educators there, especially Ms. Lapharyll Baffield, the other second grade teacher who is now a very dear friend.

Then, I went back to school to get my master's in education. When I graduated, my husband pushed me to start working for Chicago Public Schools. He said, "Sheila, you have to move on." He worked overtime at his job to put me through my master's program. I was so appreciative.

A lot of my peers at Emmanuel said, "You do not want to work at the public schools. The kids are so bad, and it's going to be so hard."

I said, "Listen. Whatever I'm doing, children are children to me. I don't care where they're at, and I can make a difference." Listening to my husband, I applied, and I got hired right away with Chicago Public Schools.

When I left Emmanuel, I went from making $21,000 to $50,000 at Caldwell.

• • • • • • •
• • • • • • • • • • •
• • • • • • • • •

I taught at Caldwell for five years. I tried to make learning fun and creative. I would create contests. If I'm teaching math, I would have students do recipes. They had to come up with their own recipes to add and subtract. Whatever recipe they had, we would have a big potluck, and the parents would come. I did a lot of things that didn't just include my classroom duties. I was in charge of the Social Committee for the staff and the Heritage Program, which is something that I started for the students in the school.

My former principal, Dr. Lucille White, said, "The only thing that really worries me about you being a leader is that you love people. When you start climbing up and growing, people will not like you and they won't be real kind to you." I said, "Well, I am not thinking about being a leader." I wasn't thinking about anything with administration. But she saw something in me.

Shelita, my daughter, went to Owen in 2000. I befriended her third-grade teacher, Ms. Conley. She knew I was a teacher teaching on the East Side. She said, "You live right around the corner from here? We have a first-grade teacher retiring. You gotta apply for Owen." I said, "No, no, no, no, no. I love my principal at Caldwell. I cannot leave her."

It was the end of the school year, and my husband and I were going to a program at Owen for my daughter. It was her awards program. I had told my husband that Shelita's teacher told me about a position. He was like, "Are you crazy? You need to apply for it. This is a great school."

As we're walking down the hallway, Mr. Kernighan (the principal) greeted us. My husband said, "Mr. Kernighan, do you still have that first-grade position available?" He said, "Yes." The principal knew that I was a teacher.

My husband said, "Let me tell you, if you hire my wife, that's going to be the best decision you've ever made."

I said, "Paul!" I hit him because I was like, *What are you doing?*

Mr. Kernighan smiled and said, "What a compliment from your husband. Mrs. Morris, are you available to come here for an interview tomorrow?"

I could not believe it. Long story short, they hired me for the position. I started at Owen in 2002.

Then, Dr. [Stanley] Griggs came [as principal] in January of 2004. At the end of 2007, he came to me because he knew that other principals were thinking about hiring me as their assistant principal. I didn't realize that. He told me, "Don't make any decisions too quickly." Some things had happened between him and the assistant principal. I think there were some issues with the commitment.

Being an administrator takes a lot of commitment. I say that for education too. If you don't have a passion for teaching and children and long hours and planning, this isn't the career for you. You have to really go into it knowing that you are going to give up a lot of your personal life and time. You are affecting the minds of other people who will be making decisions for our world. You give so much of yourself. You give a lot.

He offered me the position, which put me in such an awkward position. I was so nervous. I felt so bad because I knew that [the assistant principal] would be losing her position. Dr. Griggs and I prayed about it, and I took the position. That was my position for nine years. When he retired, he recommended me as the principal of the school.

• • • • • • •
• • • • • • • • • • •
• • • • • • • • • •

At the end of each school year, I have an exit meeting with the teachers. I always ask them, "Name five words to describe my leadership. What are some things that you think that I can do to improve my leadership and my relationship with you?" The majority of the staff members' feedback is that I'm a very compassionate leader. I was told that I am consistent. I'm strict and lovable.

When you have to make some decisions, you'll have staff members that don't like you. I think they may love me, but they might not like me. A lot of times I'm told that I take the students' side or the parents' side over theirs, but I've had to explain to them that I can't just take one side. I fight for the parents, students, and the teachers. I have to fight for all three. I want fairness.

Dr. Griggs used to tell me this. He would say, "Mrs. Morris, I know you probably feel like you're doing much more work than me, and a lot is on you." The weight of the world is on your shoulders as a principal. If anything goes wrong in the school, it doesn't matter who did it. It is always looked on [as] the principal's [responsibility].

• • • • • • •
• • • • • • • • • •
• • • • • • • • •

2020 began so great for me because my husband and I had just celebrated our thirty-fifth wedding anniversary in Mexico. It was one of the best trips ever. I felt so rejuvenated. I came back and was so excited about the new year.

After I returned to Owen, several teachers just started getting sick. It was so hard to get substitutes. I was in the classroom. The assistant principal, Ms. Kimberly Owens, was teaching. We didn't have a sub for the custodians or the teacher's aides. They weren't just absent one day. They were absent for several days.

Ms. Owens and I went into my office. We looked at each other. We both prayed together, and we just didn't know what to do. We were literally drowning. This was most of January and all of February [2020].

In March, I came to Owen on the Monday before the schools were shut down. The district emailed us packets. There were packets for every subject like reading and math. We were responsible for printing all of those packets.

I will never forget that day. We had to print over 270 packets for the kids. I had to get non-teaching staff to help me and Ms. Owens. The school would be closed by the end of the day. Parents started picking up their children early. Some parents were like, "I'm not waiting for a packet." We still had packets available for those who didn't get one. The district gave us packets that would last for a couple of weeks.

Everything was a week-by-week situation. The administration and the custodians had to stay at Owen, but the teachers were told to go home.

After three or four weeks, we had to make sure that every child had a Chromebook. We had to organize a pickup. That was something. When parents picked up Chromebooks, we had to make sure that we had masks and gloves on. Parents had to have masks as well. Some teachers volunteered to help, and we had an assembly line going. We were able to do that successfully.

The pandemic pushed Owen Scholastic Academy into the world of technology. There were a lot of schools that were well-prepared because they were using technology with teaching and learning. We were one of the schools that didn't. We had to learn very quickly. Teachers that were tech-savvy helped other teachers. We had a lot of collaboration going.

One of the biggest challenges was adjusting to being on a computer for long periods of time. It was hard to keep the students motivated. I saw a lot of sad faces when I would join an online classroom. A lot of them would turn off their cameras. It was hard to encourage the students in fifth through eighth grade to keep the cameras on. They would be in their pajamas or wearing scarves on their heads. They would put their heads down. It was sad to see them so unhappy and so detached. It was hard for me to see that.

Outside of work, my husband and I would play music. We watched movies. I talked to my mom and my dad every day. I have so many regrets because I did not hug my mom. My mother passed away in October [2020].

I did church online. I did online Bible classes every Sunday and every Wednesday. That really, really helped me to stay focused. But I would get really sad because there was so much death around me. With all of the hurts that I was going through, I still put on a face for the students and staff. I tried my hardest for them not to see what was really happening. I was crumbling.

I would talk to my daughter and grandchildren every day—not a day would go by. I send my family members a scripture and a prayer every single morning. They get that connection from me every morning, and they would respond back to me. I talk to my friends a couple of times a month. My son doesn't live with me, but I talk to him daily.

I pray that in education we are blessed with continuing to receive individuals that have passion for this line of work. Not only passion, but knowledge and intelligence so we can raise a nation. Individuals that are going to be proactive and be led by God, so that we won't have pandemics, racism, wars, and killings. Our educators are the ones that I think help to set the tone for various careers. I'm just praying that we'll have a stronger set of individuals, with a spiritual relationship, that will help to lead people to have integrity and compassion and love for mankind.

— CHAZMEIR MIXON

I just think fashion is really cool, like,
to dress like certain people do and the way the
clothes are made, their patterns, the way it fits
or the way it looks on you.

I Thought Online Was Going to be Fun

"ELENA GARCÍA," STUDENT

Elena García (not her real name) was only 12 years old at the time of this interview in October 2021, soon to be 13. She is a Chicago Public School student who, because of the rapid spreading of COVID-19 worldwide, has spent her last year doing school online away from her friends and every sense of normality she knows. She lives at home with her mother, a Spanish speaker, for whom she often finds herself translating.

Though remote learning has put a heavy weight on her shoulders, she still came to the interview smiling and excited to share her story and her dreams of entering the fashion industry when she grows up.

I FEEL LIKE WHEN COVID first started and we still went to school, I didn't really like going that much. I liked being with my friends, and I liked going to recess, lunch, stuff like that. But I thought school was really boring at first. You know, it was really difficult for me. Also, there's, like, so much drama and stuff. Girl drama, obviously. I can't really think of an example because that was in fifth grade. So I just didn't like it. And the fact I had to wake up every morning at six just to get to school? It was really, really tiring.

At first, I felt like I wanted to do online school. I didn't really want to get up early in the morning and get dressed and go to school. So when [the teacher] told us about the two weeks in online school, I was pretty happy because I had a break from it. Everybody was so excited that we had a two-week break, and I was also really excited. I thought online was going to be really fun. But then we did online school for a whole year.

It really wasn't what we thought. It was harder. Way harder. Sometimes I wouldn't get it done because I would get lazy about it and I didn't, like, have to turn it in directly to the teacher. And it was just really hard to pay attention, focus. When we took notes, I felt like it was much more than what we take in person now. I felt like homework was a lot more than what we have in person now. I had to do, like, four assignments by 11:59 from one class and some other class. It was pretty difficult because my mom usually... online, when I would leave a meeting, she will think I'm skipping school when I'm on a break or something. And for her, everything's different than how it is now. So, it was hard to explain to her.

If I had a problem with my computer, I really couldn't ask my teachers for help or tell them what's wrong. So sometimes they would mark me absent if I wasn't there because of internet problems. It was pretty bad. I would usually text my brother's girlfriend, Mina, or my brother if they could help me out with something. I didn't have internet for like two—one week? I was in summer school at that time, but we had to do it online. And, so, it was pretty hard because I missed summer school and then I couldn't really reach out to anybody 'til I went to Mina's house and used her computer to log in and stuff because they had Wi-Fi. I stayed there for a whole week, like I slept over for a whole week, and I was like, *Ahhh I miss my house!* But it was really fun to be with them.

: :

I was mostly around my mom, my brother, and my brother's girlfriend [Mina] during COVID. And my brother's girlfriend's dog. I call him Furball. I didn't see my dad during COVID as I usually did. We don't really see each other that much because he lives really far away. My mom did work a lot, so I didn't really see her during the COVID time.

My grandma, she had COVID just for a while. So did my aunt and my cousins. My aunt actually died from COVID. So did my uncle. When I found out my grandma had COVID, I was in the car with my dad and my aunt and uncle. I was actually really, really sad. I started crying, like, really out of nowhere because it impacted me really bad. Because she's old, so it was really sad. And then about my one aunt? To be honest, I wasn't so sad about it because I'm not really close to them. I'm not really close to any of my family members. It didn't really impact me that much, but it was sad to know that my family member had COVID. And about my aunt and uncle that passed away. So, I think I was at my brother's, but I didn't have a phone at that time. My dad told my mom, and my mom ended up telling me. It was actually really sad because I was close to them and they were one of my favorite uncles and aunts. I cried. I couldn't go to the funeral, though, actually. They ended up doing it in Mexico, so I couldn't go due to COVID.

Before the lockdown, I didn't get to see some friends because their parents didn't send them to school anymore. I was pretty excited to see one of my friends for the last day but then they didn't appear. I was like, *Oh my God*, because their mom said that COVID was already happening. So, I didn't really get to see some of my friends for the last time. Since I stopped seeing some friends, I kind of got distant from them, so I don't really talk to them anymore. It was, like, because of online, so we didn't really have a way to communicate so much as we did in person. I stayed in contact by either doing, like, meetings, like Zoom meetings, Google meetings, or

I would FaceTime them. I would text them. But before COVID happened, I would get to hang out with them and stuff. So it was pretty complicated, you know?

I did Photography Club during online. After school, I didn't really do anything. So, then, me and my friend were like, we should do a club, and we picked up photography because we thought it would be cool and stuff. And it was. We did like... how to take picture of, like, lights? We also did nature. If we were allowed to go outside, then we also did nature pictures. But I normally like to take pictures of my friends and stuff when we do something fun. I know in person they would give you cameras and stuff to, like, do your pictures? But during online, we had to use our phones, and if they had bad quality or something then we still had to use them. So, it was pretty different.

I didn't pick up any hobbies during COVID, but I think I followed up with the fashion trends more. That's one thing about me. I like to follow up style from, like, you know, like trending. When everybody started wearing, like, baggy... I think that's how you say it. Baggy clothes? Yeah, that's when I started following up and that's basically now my style. I used to wear skinny jeans and really tight stuff, you know? And, like, always my hair down or slicked back. But now I like my hair more down or in a clip, like right now. I used to love skinny jeans and leggings, but now I feel like I can only wear baggy jeans 'cause I feel comfortable in them.

I just think fashion is really cool, like, to dress like certain people do and the way the clothes are made, their patterns, the way it fits or the way it looks on you. After high school, my main goal is to move to New York and work for fashion or something like that. My plan is to do fashion school. And if that isn't possible, I would like to be a therapist.

In person, I like school so much better now than how I did. I actually like to do classwork now. I think it's really fun. I love taking notes—that's like my favorite thing to do. I always take colorful notes, you know? When I was still in school before COVID, compared to now, I feel like it's the same besides sometimes you have to eat in your classroom, and you can't eat in the lunchroom because another class is in it. And masks. That's really different from last year or, like, two years ago, I think. We also have to social distance. Yeah, we have to social distance. But I feel like a lot of people in my school just don't follow that and are still really, really close to each other. Especially the couples.

Photography Club isn't a choice this year now, so I didn't really do it. But then, I'm doing cheer right now. It's kind of tiring, to be honest, but it's actually pretty fun because you get to stretch out a lot, like muscles and stuff. I think we might have our first show during October or November for a fall fest at my school. And I still like to take pictures of my friends. Like, my camera roll and my snaps are just my friends. That's my thing.

I think I changed a little bit during COVID. Like, my sense of style, how I used to dress and how I dress now. Probably the way I speak too. I feel like I have more of a sense of humor. Before, I thought school was bad because I wasn't doing good. Everything just got really difficult. But now that we are in real-life school, I think it's much better and I see the difference. I'm actually learning.

— SAVANNAH GEER

Somebody That Looks Like You

LEMONE LAMPLEY, EXECUTIVE DIRECTOR

Now in his 50s, Lemone Lampley was originally raised in Southeast Chicago. After accepting a basketball scholarship and graduating with his bachelor's degree from DePaul University, he played professional basketball in Europe for eight years before returning to his hometown to work as assistant director of athletics at his alma mater, where he also earned his master's degree.

During that time, Lampley founded the not-for-profit MOCCHA, Men of Color Connected for Higher Achievement, which provides mentoring opportunities for underserved young men of color in the Chicago community. He refers to MOCCHA as his labor of love.

Lampley appeared for this Zoom interview from the dining room of his home in Frankfort, a south suburb of Chicago. Dressed in a neat, collared shirt, he was eager to talk not only about his own life, but also about the impact of 2020 on the young men of his organization and community.

He smiled and laughed often, sometimes using air quotes when speaking. When addressing racial-justice issues, he took longer pauses, repeated phrases for impact, and sometimes shook his head.

I WAS ENCOURAGED to start [MOCCHA] when I was working on my master's degree at DePaul, by one of my professors, after she saw a lot of the work that I was doing, which was pretty much geared toward mentoring young African American males. She encouraged me to start this work back in 2014, and we officially became a 501(c)(3)[80] in 2015. In May of 2016, I ended up leaving my full-time job at DePaul, where I had worked the previous eleven years as a director of development for athletics, to run this organization full time.

There's a gentleman, Steve Sarowitz[81]—he and his wife have actually helped fund MOCCHA. They saw something in me that they thought was important, and they've allowed, through their giving, for this organization to be around for five years.

---

[80] A 501(c)(3) is a nonprofit organization in US federal law, exempt from some federal income taxes. Source: https://www.501c3.org/what-is-a-501c3/

[81] Sarowitz is the founder of online payroll firm Paylocity. Source: https://www.forbes.com/profile/steven-sarowitz/?sh=577eeda543ao

I consider it a labor of love, because I was once a young African American male myself, and I know some of the pitfalls and some of the issues that they deal with. We're not the only solution, but we definitely want to be part of the solution, working with some of the underserved young men and specific communities in Chicago. For that, I'm eternally grateful.

⋮⋮⋮⋮⋮⋮ ⋯

A lot of our activities, specifically face-to-face, in person, were canceled [in 2020] due to the pandemic.

I think our last activity was late February. The Chicago Bulls hosted the all-star game down at the United Center.[82] We had a group of young men that we were able to take to that event, and then, the rest of March, the pandemic really hit hard.

We did a summer basketball camp down at East-West University [in 2019]. We were scheduled to do that [in 2020] and had to cancel. Our normal gala that always happens in October was canceled [for 2020]. Our collegiate tours to universities, we couldn't do.

For the most part, all the activities were shut down for health reasons. We tried to stay in contact with a lot of the young men via telephone calls, via online social media, things of that nature. But it really had an effect on how we operated as an organization. We had to pivot and deal with the changes that were very necessary in order to preserve health and wellness. I'm sure all other organizations had to pretty much operate under the same premise—start doing stuff online, communicating, hosting seminars, keeping the platform through social media.

In addition to the fact that [the young men] weren't able to meet with us, they were unable to meet with their friends in school. They were unable to meet with family members that maybe they were used to seeing, whether it's at a family reunion or a family gathering.

I think the socioeconomic issue was also pretty severe. A lot of parents had to go on unemployment. For a lot of the [young men in our organization], going to school was not only a place where they could get educated, it also gave them an opportunity to get breakfast and lunch. A lot of young men in underserved communities relied on those breakfast and lunch opportunities.

In general, [it was] just a very difficult year. We lost a lot of lives through COVID as well. I don't have family members that died of it, but some family members did contract it, and some close friends did pass away from COVID-related situations. It was pretty sad. It lets you know how short life can be.

---

82 The 2020 National Basketball Association All-Star Game was played on February 16, 2020, at the United Center in Chicago.

Usually, around the first or second week in October, we do a gala for our young men where we recognize those that distinguished themselves academically, athletically, socially. It also served as a fundraiser. We would have two-hundred- to three-hundred-people events, and we would give out awards.

We ended up doing something online. We did a digital discussion called, "The Effects of the Pandemic and Social Injustice, and How Has that Affected African Americans?" We had some very prominent people [as] featured speakers on the panel. We had Rashard Johnson, who is the president and CEO of the Advocate Hospitals.[83] We had a gentleman named David Booth, who is the vice president of operations for the NBA.[84] Then also a local gentleman named Bob Hawkinson, who owns the Kia Hawkinson dealership out in the south suburbs.[85] We discussed different things that affected us throughout the year—very fruitful.

I thought the digital discussion was very informative because we had a president who was in charge of a whole hospital staff, Mr. Rashard Johnson. And definitely [hospital workers'] lives were changed by an inrush of people with COVID, and dealing with those that are on the front lines to try and get people healed, while still trying to protect themselves.

He dealt with that, and he as a leader, specifically an African American leader, was able to work through that and still come out pretty good. It was just a heroic effort. In that panel discussion, we showed that despite what was going on, you can still make a difference in your area. Wherever you are, you can still be a voice for social injustice.

In fact, that's one of the reasons we had David Booth. The NBA allow[ed] a lot of the athletes to utilize their platform. They had opportunities to be interviewed by media sportscasters. They talked about some of the social injustice that went on or that they've seen.

[Athletes] were allowed to—in lieu of having their names on the back of their jerseys—put clauses like "Black Lives Matter," "Justice." Then [painted] on the court, they have Black Lives Matter.

83 Rashard Johnson is president of both Advocate Trinity Hospital, in Chicago, and Advocate South Suburban Hospital, in Hazel Crest, IL, which are part of Advocate Health Care, the 10th largest not-for-profit, integrated health system in the United States. Source: https://www.nmqf.org/40-under-40-awardees/2020/rashard-johnson

84 David Booth's official title is NBA vice president, Basketball Operations. Source: https://www.nba.com/news/malik-rose-david-booth-nba-vice-presidents-official-release

85 Bob Hawkinson is the owner/managing partner of Kia Hawkinson in Matteson, Illinois. Source: https://hawkinsonkia.com/sales-team

The NBA allowed even their coaches, Black and white, [to] come out and speak about some of the well-documented cases. Breonna Taylor down in Kentucky, obviously George Floyd.

I can still remember, they interviewed the coach of the San Antonio Spurs. His name is Popovich. Caucasian guy.[86] He came out and said some very strong things. He said [that] to see what happened to George Floyd, as a white person, didn't make him feel good at all.

Despite the tragedies that we saw, it gave America an opportunity to [address] some of the realities that we are facing as a country, in a divided country.

I think that if you are just human, you could see some of the things that took place were just really, in my opinion, not right.

A lot of times, out of negative things, positive results come. To actually see footage of George Floyd being killed on national TV, even though it's pretty grotesque, America saw it. We saw it. We saw what happened with Breonna Taylor. We saw so many other killings that took place throughout the country.

It gave us an opportunity and a platform to discuss issues that we really need to discuss. Not just as Black Americans, not just as white Americans, but as just human people, trying to make choices that we think are going to better influence us and progress going forward.

Before technology came on the scene, in terms of being able to actually video-record incidents, we heard a lot about injustices, but we couldn't see it. But now, with the advent of the smartphone and the cameras, we can actually see what is taking place in some cases.

I don't remember where I was [when I heard about George Floyd's murder], but I do know that when I got a chance to see some of the footage—[it was] very disturbing.

It's hard to watch a man calling out for his life and just having his life snuffed out by somebody that says they serve and protect. It wasn't good. And then the Breonna Taylor case in Louisville, Kentucky, came out, and what we heard or saw from that case wasn't good as well.

86 Gregg Popovich, head coach/president of the San Antonio Spurs NBA basketball team.
Source: https://www.nba.com/spurs/gregg-popovich

And I want to be specifically clear: I don't think all policemen are bad, Black or white. I don't think mankind itself is all bad, Black or white.

People say, "This isn't an America we know." Well, if you look at history, it is. This is the America we know. And we've seen it countless times throughout history, where things happened that really shouldn't happen.

I think once we come to grips with what the reality of the situation is, we can better deal with it. Unfortunately, sometimes we turn a deaf ear to it, or we put on our blinders and we say, "It's not real. It's fake news." But it's not.

We've heard about it, but now to actually see it, we get a snapshot of some of the injustice. And I think that if we're all going to live together, and as peacefully as we can, we need to realize that there does need to be changes made in terms of the laws in this country, some that are not fair and just.

I'm gonna be honest. You feel anger, you feel rage, especially when it's somebody that looks like you.

Seeing those images [of George Floyd], they weren't good. You got him pinned down, he can't do anything, and then I think what's more disturbing than that is that you got three or four other officers that are on the scene and they're just sitting there as well. They're the co-conspirators, or they're complicit with what's going on.

This man is calling out for his life. You've got people screaming, "Let him up! Let him go! Get off of him! He's not doing anything!" And this officer just— I think it's anywhere from eight to ten minutes that he had his knee on the guy's neck, basically killed him right there. I don't know [how] much more you need to see or say when you see something like that.

Where is your compassion? I mean, this guy is a crook? OK, arrest him, put him in handcuffs, put him in a car, move forward.

Just makes you feel helpless, you know. Like, really? This is where America has gotten to? I think it was just disturbing. That would be the word. If I could use any word, it was disturbing to see that. Disturbing.

I support the right to protest, but in a lawful way. I in no way support opportunists who go out and loot and steal, maim people, bust windows of innocent business owners for no reason other than you're upset and/or you're there to steal and rob.

I will say this: I think that a lot of times when you have people that feel oppressed, and they feel that there's not going to be change, you put them into a situation where they force themselves to do stuff that's not right. And they know it's not right, but they feel, "This is the only retribution I'm going to get."

Negative things get the most public space on television or social media. But it's not the right way to handle situations, and in no way do I justify anybody that's out there looting or burglarizing or setting stuff on fire, all in the sacred name of "protest."

That's not a peaceful protest. I don't think that does anything beneficial for those people that feel oppressed. I think there is a better way to handle it.

It takes away from the real issues that need to be dealt with. We saw a lot of tragedy happen in this country. Specifically, toward the end, with what happened down in DC at the Capitol.[87]

I'm hoping that, going forward, we as a people can do better. There's a saying in the world, "When you know better, you do better." And we do know that there needs to be some things done a lot differently than we saw in 2020.

I think people have to get out and vote—not only at the national level, but at the local level—[for] those officials that are running for office. Investigate, do your research, see what laws that they're enacting. I think the polls are one way that we can help change things that are happening in America.

People that were fed up with the past administration, they went out and voted in numbers to make change. I'm hoping for a good change.

∴∴∴∴

I'm actually looking to have a Zoom conference with some of our young men from MOCCHA, and one of the things we'll be looking to discuss is, how has the pandemic, as well as the social injustice that we've seen, affected them, specifically as young men of color.

It was something that we faced as a world that we didn't see coming. How we acted or responded to that, trying to help save lives and make lives better for people of all creeds and color, is going to come through an act of passion, love.

---

[87] On January 6, 2021, Trump supporters stormed the U.S. Capitol to object to the counting of electorial votes from the 2020 election. Source: https://www.usatoday.com/story/news/nation/2021/01/06/capitol-hill-riot-heres-everything-we-know/6573033002/

I still believe that out of this difficulty that we've seen, there are going to be some very positive things that happen afterwards. I would encourage not just our young men, but all the other young African American males to continue to have a hope, keep your dream, and work hard.

Hard work always pays off. My dad always told me that as a young man.

I would say [to the young people] that despite the negativity you've seen [over the pandemic], continue to aspire to succeed. I think the opportunities are there, and don't let one specific time in your life hold you back from accomplishing what your dream is. Continue to pursue your dream despite the pandemic and the social unrest that you've seen in 2020. Because I think if you do, on the other side of that, you're going to see a brighter path, a brighter future for yourself.

— CHRISTY MARGESON

I'm a workaholic, so to be out of work for those few months from March until September [2020], that was a new experience for me.

History Repeats Itself

"MYRNA," JOURNALIST

Myrna—who asked that we use a pseudonym—is a 24-year-old journalist of Mexican and Puerto Rican descent. She intended to leave for the Peace Corps' pre-service training in March 2020, but her two-year plan to teach English as a foreign language in a small Eastern-European country was abruptly canceled. She is still unsure of her departure date.

During the interview, she sat in a spare room, empty except for a desk and bed, in her grandparents' house in the Humboldt Park neighborhood. During the COVID-19 pandemic, Humboldt Park's Latinx, undocumented, and senior populations have significantly struggled to manage outbreaks of the virus.[88] Myrna hopes that with time and security, she can rent an apartment of her own in a safer neighborhood in the city.

I HAVE THIS BAD HABIT. Like, the first thing I do when I wake up is check my phone. [That morning] I hadn't even sat up in bed. I rolled over, grabbed my phone, and saw that I had a missed call. I'm not sure what time I had woken up. It was probably about 9 a.m. or 10 a.m. and I saw that, like, an hour or two earlier I had a missed phone call. I didn't recognize the number. It just said "Washington, DC," and my first thought was, it's something for the Peace Corps.

So, I immediately called the number back. A lady picked up. "We're not sending anyone anywhere."

March 11, the night before, I had gone out with my friends to say goodbye to them and hang out for the last time. We went to this place called Avondale Tap. It's a bar in the neighborhood. It was four of us and we just went there to really hang out. We ate food, got a drink. One of my friends got into knitting, so I asked her to make me a frog because she had started making little figures. She surprised me with it that night. I still have it. It was meant for me to take [with me on my assignment].

I was just thinking of the *coquí*. It's a little frog that's native to Puerto Rico. I have family members that have frogs everywhere in the house because people from Puerto Rico really care about the *coquí*.

---

88 The zip codes comprising the Humboldt Park neighborhood have consistently reported some of the highest case counts in Chicago. Source: https://data.cityofchicago.org/widgets/yhhz-zm2v?mobile_redirect=true

I don't think anyone was wearing a mask [at Avondale Tap]. What I do remember was the owner, or one of the bartenders, was making an announcement using a microphone. I don't remember what the announcement was, but they ended it with a reminder for everyone to wash their hands and stay safe. I don't even think I was super worried about it because, during that time, I still didn't think it was that serious in the US.

I hated when the night ended and I had to hug them all goodbye. That sucked. But I was still kind of holding on to the excitement of leaving. It was just bittersweet. So, yeah, I had that tearful goodbye and then the morning after I was like, "Well, I'm not going anywhere."

. . . .
. . . .

My mom passed away when I was four. I've always just dealt with it. It's just a day-to-day thing I have to live with. I mean, I think about it every day just because she's my mother. The day I was supposed to leave for the Peace Corps would have been her birthday.

[On] my dad's side of the family, the Puerto Rican side, no one really travels a lot outside of going to Puerto Rico. I don't know many people at all in my family that have traveled outside of the country, and if they do, it's just for vacation. So for me to go overseas, that was a big deal for them, because I didn't know the language. I didn't know anyone there. I had never been out of the country before.

It's different for them just going to Puerto Rico, because we know people there. We know the language. So I think the circumstances were different enough for them to be like, "Wow, she's doing that."

No one in my family really understood why I wanted to do it. I was kind of the odd one out. I'm sure there's some Peace Corps volunteers that know other people who have [volunteered] or at least something similar, or at least had family who maybe didn't have those experiences but supported them. I didn't have a lot of that.

Might have been a month later, me and my grandparents had some family over for dinner. My great-grandma came. She came to say "hi" to me in my bedroom and she's like, "Oh, you're not going?" And I was like, "No, I'm not." She kind of nodded her head. She was like, "Don't go." She didn't want me to go because she was so worried for me. She was a little bit happy, not because of COVID, but because [my leaving] was delayed. In my family, that was the consensus, that they were relieved that I would be here longer.

[I felt] a little bit of everything—relieved because I had a lot of anxiety with getting on the plane and starting my service, a little bit bummed because it was delayed, because I was also excited to start. The main thing was just the shock of it all. That something so big can happen that would change everything and change such a big plan that seemed so cemented. Or at least it seemed so cemented to me. And just the worry of, like, how long are things going to be this bad? Are they going to be worse? You know, the fear of the unknown.

I think I've only been on a plane once or twice, but I was probably about four years old, maybe three. So, very young. I don't even have any memory of being on a plane. I just know that from family stories because we went to Florida to visit family.

I was supposed to be teaching English as a foreign language. I was incredibly nervous. I was just kind of like, *How is this going to work?* Even just the thought of going to the airport was like, *Where do I go? What should I do?* Like, Who do I talk to? And then the idea of getting through an airport in [my host country] was even more frightening. Nerve-wracking. I barely spoke the language.

In January of 2020, I had started taking language courses a couple of times a week to start learning the basics of [my host country's language]. That way, when we did get to the country, we could at least say hello to people or express basic needs, introduce ourselves, just to get us by, until we continued the language courses once we were there.

● ● ● ● ● ● ●
● ● ● ● ● ● ● ● ● ● ● ●
● ● ● ● ● ● ● ● ●

I think the pandemic, for most people, caused them to slow down a bit. I'm a work-aholic, so to be out of work for those few months from March until September [2020], that was a new experience for me. I've always been working on something. It was nice to have that free time. But when September 2020 came, I was starting to feel bored and stir-crazy. So that's when I started working in retail.

I learned everything that retail and food service people go through, especially now during a pandemic with people not wanting to comply with the precautions and the mandates. I was fortunate enough to not have to deal with too much of that, but obviously there was a little bit of, you know, having to remind customers to put on masks, people being more irritable.

I've [also] been more strategic with my news consumption. Before I graduated college and before the start of the pandemic, I was consuming as much as possible. My Instagram, my Twitter, my LinkedIn—all my social media—I was following as many news organizations as possible. And that was just because I figured, I'm a journalist, I have to be as aware of everything that's going on as possible.

But as time went on, I was like, *I need to find a way where I'm not consuming so much,* because it did get stressful. At one point it was like, *Everything's negative.* Now, I follow most of my news organizations on Facebook, and then I [subscribe to] a few email newsletters. But, like, Twitter is a very specific news organization that I follow just for work. Instagram, I try to keep as fun as possible as well as YouTube. It's pretty much for entertainment purposes and to relieve some stress and just pass the time, no longer to consume news like [I] used to.

I also started therapy last year, so that's been really helpful. I didn't have anything against therapy; it's an app. I just never really felt like I needed it myself before the pandemic.

A lot of [my decision to try therapy] came from the fact that it seemed like more people were doing it. A lot more people were being open about mental health and talking about it, so it just felt easier. I wanted some more guidance. I was also struggling with the stress of trying to communicate with some of my family members the seriousness of COVID. And it's kind of hard when you're having a conversation with someone and you're trying your hardest to remain calm. If the conversation isn't going where you want it, you're feeling frustrated and everything.

⁜

My plan before the pandemic was to do the Peace Corps—finish my two years of service—and then go to grad school. Now, I'm still trying to decide if I want to do grad school right now or if I want to wait. I'm not sure if I'm ready to start up school again. I'm pretty happy with where I'm at in my life right now.

I've tried to focus on the good things during this whole pandemic, because everything seems so negative all the time. A highlight would be my current job. That was a big moment for me and something that I was really happy about.

Other than that, my birthday. I was really happy just to be alive. It didn't feel like a regular birthday. I felt more grateful for it. You know, obviously a lot of people didn't get the chance to see their next birthday, so I think just, like, any time I get to spend with my family is always the highlight.

My whole Peace Corps experience will definitely stick with me, whether or not I end up serving. The idea of getting accepted and all the preparation, and then obviously the delay in service because of the pandemic—they'll stick with me forever because it was such a huge time in my life, and I was preparing so much for it physically and mentally.

I'll remember because the pandemic was happening, but also the riots and the huge conversations about race and police brutality. That was so big. When I was going through that time period, it really reminded me of 1968 because so much happened during that year. During that summer, I kept replaying the saying, "History repeats itself." Cause I literally feel like we're reliving, like, so many things that we had already experienced.

The summer of 2020, I'll remember forever. It was a very crazy time.

—UKIAH MOOSES

Limbs of a Whole

SALOUMEH BOZORGZADEH, PSYCHOLOGIST

Saloumeh Bozorgzadeh is a psychologist and therapist in Chicago who splits her time between a practice with Evolve Wellness and the Sufi Psychology Association, which she calls her passion project. Her private practice is located on the North Side of Chicago, where she specializes in mood disorders, relationship issues, and self-harm. Her work with the Sufi Psychology Association has made a large impact in communities affected by the pandemic. Initiatives like "Caring for Our Caregivers," which teaches healthcare workers how to use meditative practices to better their mental health, has been covered in media sources like the Chicago Tribune.[89]

Bozorgzadeh said it's difficult for her to sit comfortably knowing that someone else is struggling. This is especially true considering her background in Sufism,[90] a mystical ascetic form of Islam that studies self-knowledge and the idea that there is more to individuals than their circumstances.

Though she said it has been difficult to find a balance between her personal and professional life during the pandemic, her community-service work has grounded her.

I FEEL LIKE AT THE END of February [2020] we knew something was coming around. I don't remember how I even heard about it. I was in Northern California giving a lecture, and then I came back. So basically, I think it was mid-March when I first heard about the virus.

I have a group practice. We shut down right then and there and went virtual. We opened [in person] a little bit before this Delta variant,[91] and that was great, but once the mask mandates went into effect again, we closed back up. Mostly because with therapy it's hard to get the full effect with the mask. So now I'm home maybe one or two days out of the week. I'll just go into the office and do virtual sessions from the office just to get out, but we're still home 100 percent right now.

---

89 Source: https://www.chicagotribune.com/lifestyles/ct-xpm-2012-11-28-sc-health-1128-mental-health-caregiving-20121128-story.html

90 Source: https://www.nytimes.com/2017/11/24/world/middleeast/sufi-muslim-explainer.html

91 The Delta variant of COVID-19 began to dominate US cases in the summer of 2021. Source: https://www.webmd.com/lung/news/20210712/what-to-know-about-COVID-delta-variant

For a lot of the younger clients, who are more comfortable with things online, they like it, especially if this is their first introduction to therapy. It also allows for more flexibility. Before people could come after work or on weekends. Those were prime slots. But now, being virtual, people can do it on their lunch break, whenever they have a chance throughout the day.

The [patients] who started out in person had a harder time going virtual. There's a different kind of dynamic that happens in person. There's so much more to sessions than just sitting at home. It's them getting out of their space, coming to the office. It feels safe and comforting for them there. Those clients were, and still are, constantly asking, "When do we go back? When do we go back?" It feels less formal when you're doing therapy from your home environment. Like I once had a client who made a comment about something in my house that she could see. It's a little strange.

We didn't know how long this was going to last. What's gonna happen? What do we do? It was this uncertainty. That was the issue that was forefront on clients' minds, and there was an increased level of anxiety in the world. So not only were they thinking it, but me, as a therapist, I'm having the same thoughts. How do I lead you or help you through something if I'm right in there with you? Typically, in therapy when someone would come in, they might be talking about stressors they're going through. You're outside of that without your own feelings and emotions coloring your perspective. You have more of a neutral view, which I think was hard to do [during the pandemic], so therapists were really burning out. For the first time, there wasn't the separation of what your client was going through. We were right there in the same boat, which makes it very challenging in terms of keeping a neutral perspective.

• • • • • • • •
• • • • • • • • • • • •
• • • • • • • •

My personal life really halted. My friends were very fearful, and so they stayed inside. We wouldn't even see each other outside much. So, in terms of my personal life and professional life, it was imbalanced. I didn't have anybody around me, except for my dog. But you can only hang out with your dog so much.

I felt like I couldn't have Zoom meetings with my friends or talk to them because I would feel that they were stressed out, and I didn't have the capacity to take on any more people's problems. Your friends are your escape, and *that* was stressful. So, I couldn't even do that.

Once I was able to take some time to figure out where I stand with my thoughts about the pandemic and how I'm coping with it, it became a little easier. But in the beginning, [I] was just being very reactive. Nobody knew what was happening. Clients had their concerns, and I had the same ones, right?

With my friends it probably wasn't until this year when things began to settle down and open up a little bit. Some of that panic energy kind of dissipated and it became a lot easier to be around people.

I think some of the practices [we teach] really helped. One was meditation practices in terms of turning inward, because everything around you was stressful. It was the election. There were all the social causes. There were the wildfires. There were aliens, apparently.[92] Everywhere you looked externally for peace, you weren't going to get it.

So my own meditative practice picked up, and that really helped. I also think if it wasn't for this initiative with Sufi Psychology, where I was so busy, I would have felt the emptiness a lot more. I think it would have played a big role in where I would be at now, in terms of mental health. You got out of your head, you got out of your anxiety. You got out of just thinking about yourself.

....
::::::::::....
....

Sufi Psychology Association is based out of California, but we're nationwide. We're doing workshops, events, and donations. We have our Instagram. We've got a lot of resources like "Monthly Wellness Live" talks about how to bring some balance into your life. Or when kids started returning to school and parents were really stressed out, we created something called "Back to School Mondays," professionals providing tips every week for parents.

It was in March [2020] when the Sufi Psychology Association put together something called "Coping with the COVID Crisis," because we started realizing that people were anxious. They were really scared.

[It] was a free online class, essentially. Every two days a professional—whether it's a psychologist or a physician—will give tips on how people can cope with what they're feeling. That was available for the public. We kept up with that probably till about August or September [2020].

In April [2020] is when we began the "Caring for Our Caregivers" initiative. Prior to the pandemic, we were doing a lot of work on burnout with health workers because they have the highest rate of suicide of any profession, and that was before COVID. So when COVID hit we were scared about what they were going through.

We started donating electronic tablets that we had loaded with proven evidence-based stress-relieving techniques. We started donating them to hospitals with individually wrapped disposable headsets so that they can put it in their break

---

92 A US military report released in June 2021 would not rule out the existence of aliens as the cause of several UFO sightings by military aircraft.

room or the wellness rooms for the staff. We started here in Chicago, and by the end of the year we were in over three hundred hospitals and fifty states, and four countries.

We were just trying to give as much as we could. Once we heard back from a hospital that said, "Our nurses love the tablets. They're using them. They keep asking for them. Can you donate to our sister hospital? We think they need it." And we're like, "Oh my gosh, it's helping!" We heard back from another nurse who said, "Everyone keeps asking for this; this is better than the pizza that we keep getting." One place was really lovely; we had called about a donation, and as we were donating to them, the woman said, "You know, my daughter's a nurse in a different state. I know she's really burned out. They could really use it there." Every time there was an article written about what we were doing, we would get emails from nurses from all over the nation. I remember the first time that happened, we got an email from a nurse in West Virginia who said, "How do we get on this list? Is there any way you can donate to us? We need this." And it was so amazing. When they started reaching out, I think that's when it solidified that something is happening here.

There's a poem by a Persian poet named Sa'adi. It's actually a poem they have at the United Nations. It says: "Human beings are limbs of a whole. If one limb is suffering, you can't call yourself human."[93] So, part of the Sufi philosophy is also that fact that we are part of this greater whole.

I can't sit comfortably if I know that someone else is struggling. We were doing it for everyone else, but I have to say, each and every one of us gained a benefit.

∴∴∴∴∴∴
∴∴∴∴∴∴ ∴∴
∴∴∴∴∴∴∴

It's been a balance trying to do both [Sufi Psychology and a private practice], especially during COVID. A lot of old clients returned because everyone was so stressed. At first, our patient population decreased, mostly because people were losing their jobs. They were very concerned about insurance and whether they would be able to maintain therapy. And then, once the executive order[94] went

---

[93] The poem by Sa'adi (c. 1184–1292) appears as an inscription with a carpet, a gift from Iran. One translation from the Persian reads:

> Adam's children are limbs of one body
> That in creation are made of one gem.
> When life and time hurt a limb,
> Other limbs will not be at ease.
> You who are not sad for the suffering of others,
> Do not deserve to be called human.

[94] Governor J.B. Pritzker issued Executive Order 2020–09 in March 2020 expanding access to telehealth services for Illinois residents. Source: https://www2.illinois.gov/Pages/Executive-Orders/ExecutiveOrder 2020-09.aspx

in, all sorts of opportunities opened up. So, they were able to continue therapy. A lot of people returned.

It got pretty busy, but I was able to balance them. You know, just making sure that I'm scheduling my time appropriately, certain days going towards the Sufi Psychology Association and other days going towards my own private practice.

One of the things we were focusing on was a meditation method called Tamarkoz. Basically, this is a meditative practice that has five different components. One of them is mind relaxation, which is similar to mindfulness. There's deep breathing exercises, meditative movements, visualization concentration practices. So basically, we started using that because it was researched and used at [University of California]-Berkeley, [University of California]-Davis, Kaiser Permanente. It's been researched to show it decreases perceived stress and increases positive emotion in times of stress.

So, we started putting that [into the tablets], because that way healthcare workers could also pick what works. That's the main thing that we've been recommending and using, because you can pick what works for you.

Being able to do some of those exercises would be wonderful for people to slowly quiet their minds, get a little bit more control, to learn to focus themselves, to just be in a state of being and without any expectations. Just to be happy and content with where they are. That's a lot of what Tamarkoz teaches.

Tamarkoz stems from a Sufi philosophy. The entire goal of Sufism is for each person to know themselves. So it's a lot of experiential meditative practices. Kind of sorting through, "What have I gathered from the world? What are these narratives I tell myself?" It's like trying to get to the root of who you are. [Sufism is] knowing the incredible strength that you have within and therefore not relying on your emotions to define a moment for you.

. . . .
. . . .
. . . .

[The pandemic] is good for the mental health field because it's getting rid of some of the lingering stigma. The United States is pretty far along, probably further than other countries, in accepting mental health as being legitimate. I feel like in workplaces too, employers are becoming more aware that this is an issue. The landscape of therapy is changing.

Before, rarely did people have virtual sessions. Now we are forced to have virtual sessions. I think it's probably going to continue.

The other interesting thing: I think this time forced people to evaluate their lives and sit with themselves. I think part of that is very challenging and difficult. There might be a lot of stuff that has popped up that is very difficult, and they need help with that.

On the other end of that, I think this pandemic is really going to be the turning point in our history where people shift how they live. It might not be so quick and go, go, go, but people are going to try to live a little bit more balanced and take a little more time for themselves.

One of the most important things [for people struggling with mental health] is tapping into whatever it is that inspires you and keeps you going. I think everybody has something. For some people, it's their faith; for some, it's connecting with nature. I think it's finding that thing that gets you motivated and gets you moving.

The most important thing is to have hope. When hope dissipates, that's when we're in trouble. So whatever we can do to kind of inspire hope. It might not be easy. You might not be laughing and giggling your way through it. That's OK. But as long as you don't lose hope, I think that's the most important thing.

—ZOEY FINK

The Silent Pandemic

MEGAN BENNETT, COMMUNICATIONS MANAGER

Megan Bennett came to the Greater Chicago Food Depository in search of a job with meaning. The Food Depository's mission—to provide food to people in need, as well as to end hunger and its root causes in the greater Chicago area—made it a clear draw. She began working at the Food Depository as a communicator and interviewer in late 2019, only a few months before the COVID-19 pandemic hit the United States.

The Food Depository partners with hundreds of pantries, soup kitchens, shelters and similar programs through-out Cook County to supply them with the food they need.

I REMEMBER WHEN those first shutdowns happened in March 2020, we all went home and thought it was going to be two weeks. We knew then that there was going to be a heightened demand for food assistance because there were people who were going to be out of work. Children weren't going to be in school, and a lot of children rely on free or reduced-price meals at school. People were not going to be paid, and people might lose their jobs.

I don't think any of us could have seen what it was going to become, but over those first couple of months, the magnitude of the need was heartbreaking. We knew that we had a system in place, but we've never seen anything quite like this before. The Food Depository has been around for forty-two years now, and our organization has never seen a crisis quite like this.

The experience of going to a pantry has really evolved in the last several decades. A lot of what we saw before the pandemic was people going through aisles of food, picking things up off shelves. It's a very personal experience. There's a pantry that I remember going to my first week at the Food Depository, and every single person that came in got a hug from one of the volunteers.

Those types of things couldn't happen anymore, so people had to figure out [how the new system would work]. "OK, how are we going to deliver?" or "How are we going to serve this heightened need?" "What's the most efficient way to do that?" So we saw people come up with a lot of creative solutions. Of course, we gave guidelines about social distancing and outdoor distribution, but people had to figure out how that was going to work for them.

Luckily, a majority of our partners were able to stay open, but they had to figure out, like, "OK, if we're gonna do it outside, we can do a drive-through, so we can stay outdoors for as long as we can." But then, of course, in the winter it got a little bit more difficult. Doing it outdoors, figuring out how to socially distance, figuring out how to do prepacked bags and boxes when before people [were] going in with their shopping carts—it really altered the distribution model as well as what kind of food they were getting.

So then, to kind of alleviate some of the demand on some of our partners, we also started doing pop-up distributions in some of our high-need areas. The South and West Sides particularly were hit hardest by not only the virus itself, but also by the food insecurity that grew out of the pandemic, and those were neighborhoods and areas that were already disproportionately impacted by poverty and food insecurity before. So, we were doing pop-ups in those areas, and we would see like five hundred to a thousand people come per pop-up.

I remember I went to one of those pop-ups in one of the early months of the pandemic in Washington Park on the South Side. I was on the Dan Ryan[95] trying to get off the exit, and the exit was totally backed up. I was like, "Oh, there must have been an accident or something."

It wasn't an accident; it was the line of people trying to get their car to the drive-through pop-up. I've never in my life seen anything like that.

· · · · · · ·
· · · · · · · · · · ·
· · · · · · · · ·

We saw an impact on our work not only from the partner side but from our benefits outreach team, the people who connect others to SNAP[96] and Medicaid. In the early months, they were getting record numbers of calls, ten times what they were seeing before. People were scared; they didn't know what to do. I spoke to a lot of people during that period that were experiencing food insecurity for the first time: people that worked in the service industry, people that left their jobs because they had health issues.

---

95 The Dan Ryan Expressway is the name for the combined I-90 and I-94 interstates from Chicago's Loop south to I-57.
96 The Supplemental Nutrition Assistance Program provides aid to low-income families to buy healthy food. Source: https://www.fns.usda.gov/snap/supplemental-nutrition-assistance-program

We saw our benefits outreach change, our job training had to change. We [used to have] a fourteen-week program that was back-of-the-house culinary training. People were in the commercial kitchen, in these tight spaces doing this work side-by-side. Couldn't do that anymore, so we had to switch to a hybrid. Now we're looking at other ways to train people in other industries.

Then, with our volunteer department, we had to figure out how to keep volunteers in here safely. Volunteers come in nearly every day to help pack food, but we had to think about how to socially distance them, what are the most needed things right now. As health advisories evolved, we've evolved with them. We did extra cleaning of our facilities; we still do all these things. But having to very quickly figure out what that's going to look like for us, how to keep people safe, both at our partners' and in our facility, it really just turned everything upside down.

In the wake of all that, as we were still kind of navigating it, as we saw a lot of things change, we've also seen a lot of people step up. We've seen donations increase. People realizing that there are others in their community who don't have enough on the table.

Just to put it into a little bit of perspective numbers-wise, between February 2020 and February 2021, we distributed 30 percent more pounds of food compared to the same time period prior. That amounts to about 22.3 million additional meals from right before the shutdowns happened through the first few months of 2021.

In 2021, we've seen that kind of level out, but even now it's still nowhere near pre-pandemic levels. We're seeing the economic fallout of this pandemic still, and we're going to be seeing the economic fallout of this pandemic for months and even years to come.

• • • • • • • •
• • • • • • • • • • •
• • • • • • • • • •

I remember talking to someone at a food pantry not long ago, probably in June of [2021], that they had gone through three separate jobs in the midst of the pandemic. They worked in the food service industry, and I remember them talking about how they got one job, but then it closed, and then they got another one, and then that closed too, and then they got one at the airport, but there were less flights. Luckily by the time I talked to them they were going back to one of their original jobs later that month, but that was super stressful for them. There [were] a lot of people that were going through similar things where you just felt like you couldn't catch a break.

We want them to know there's always going to be a place that they can go for food, and that there's always going to be someone there for them. I think that, from the people I've spoken to at different sites, that is something that gives them a lot of peace and a lot of ease.

In April of 2020, as we realized this was going to be a very long-term crisis, I started making calls to some of our food-pantry partners. Out of that I met a pastor at one of our partner churches in Roseland, the Allen Metropolitan Community Church. He talked about this increase that they were seeing in demand for the hot-meal program they would do Wednesdays. He told me that before the pandemic, people from different nursing homes or different group-home facilities would be bused into their church. Every Wednesday they would come get a meal. There would be people playing live music. It was just really special, the way he was describing it. It sounded like such a special, intimate time of community and sharing a meal together.

Of course, that went away after the pandemic began. The people went away, but the volunteers there, the pastor, and the entire church congregation, they didn't go away. What they started doing was making these to-go meals, hundreds of hundreds of meals every Wednesday. They would take meals to those group homes and senior citizen centers that were once coming to them. They ended up delivering way more than before the pandemic.

I met one of the volunteers there, a woman in about her late 60s or early 70s who's one of the leaders that was taking meals to the folks on her block. She told me about how she grew up on the same block that she was volunteering on, and so these older folks that helped raise her, she was now finding a way to take care of them. It was a really beautiful kind of full-circle moment, seeing the way that they were taking care of each other. Sometimes they would leave notes for her as she was leaving, because obviously they couldn't meet in person. Within a week or so, they were able to flip the switch.

In the beginning of the pandemic, the local hospital in Roseland had to shut their kitchen down, so on Wednesdays, that same church would make meals for the people at the hospital. They helped with that until the hospital was able to get back up and running. It was just so cool to see how they were trying to help where they could in ways that would never have been needed before.

A lot of our partners that I've spoken to have mentioned, "I wish I could see people's faces like I used to," "I wish I could give people hugs like I used to," "I wish that I knew everyone's name that was coming through the door." A lot of that's impossible now, but luckily a lot of the places that I've seen in the last year and a half, they're really trying to keep that personal touch. They're really trying to find ways to connect with people through these extra barriers. There is still that effort, there's still that care, there's still that love. I mean, there has to be, or else people wouldn't be doing this, especially now. But the fact that they're still there and still helping to lift up their community— It is a labor of love for sure.

I think that's one of the great things about food, right? It's something that's a community builder. It brings people together. We say all the time in this work that "food is love, food is family, food is connection," and it brings people together. We're still [trying] to embody that in a lot of different ways.

• • • • • • •
• • • • • • • • • •
• • • • • • • • • •

We saw a lot of the unrest in our communities as a result of the killing of George Floyd [in May 2020]. Some people for the first time were seeing and understanding how systemic racism fuels so many different socioeconomic issues, including food insecurity, including poverty. We saw people understanding for the first time something that we've seen for a long time, that systemic racism and injustice is a root cause of and plays a direct role in hunger for so many people.

In those first couple of days after the killing, there were protests and there were a lot of areas in the city closed. That meant that some of our food pantries had to close, so we had to figure out how we were going to get in these communities to make sure everyone had the food they needed. Luckily, we were able to still get on the roads and be able to serve people, but that was something that we had to think about and adjust to quickly.

It was such an emotional time for not only our organization, but also a lot of the partners we serve and the areas of the city that we serve. We can't talk about food insecurity or food justice or eliminating hunger without talking about this huge, huge part of it. Racial equity is something that our organization has talked about for a long time, and it's something that we've been dedicated to for a while, so of course in the middle of the pandemic, when people were seeing these disproportionate impacts of not only the virus but the economic changes it brought, it led to a lot of conversations starting.

We've started offering grant funding to partner sites, particularly in Black and brown communities. So far, we've given away millions of dollars to help them transform their operations and serve more people by strengthening the food safety net in these communities as well as opening up new food pantries in these areas. When I talk about transforming operations, I'm talking about building new shelving, adding cold storage so they can serve more fruits and vegetables, building accessible entryways. During the pandemic, and especially at the time of the racial justice movements, we saw the conversation build in new ways around these ideas of racial equity and how they impact food insecurity.

There's still a lot of work to do. There's still more that needs to be done; just acknowledging it is not enough. There needs to be action behind it. We have to find tangible ways to address food justice, and there cannot be food justice without racial justice.

I think one of the most important things to remember is that, while the pandemic highlighted and worsened a lot of the need that we're seeing in our community, there was already a lot of need before then. We talk a lot about this kind of silent pandemic that was going on long before March 2020. So many areas of our city and our county were already facing these massive rates of food insecurity. Even after the worst of this pandemic is behind us, they'll still be recovering.

The goal should not be getting back to pre-pandemic levels. We want to live in a world where no one is going hungry, where no one has food insecurity. We should want to be better than where we were. We should want to be ensuring that everyone has adequate access to the food they need. There's a lot more work to do, even after the pandemic is over and done with. That's what I want people to think about, because the pandemic didn't cause the issues, it just made them worse. It's important to get into it and start dealing with it, because it's not going to happen if nobody starts talking about it.

—RUBEN ROJAS

A Blessing and a Curse

MIRZA BAIG, COLLEGE STUDENT

Mirza Baig is a 22-year-old sophomore in college. He lives in Skokie, a middle-class suburb near Chicago, with his family. At the time of this interview, he was attending Oakton Community College in nearby Des Plaines and looking forward to transferring to DePaul University in the spring of 2022.

Baig works part time as a shift leader at Walgreens. From the beginning of the pandemic, he picked up extra shifts in order to provide financial support to his family. He and his mother were the only ones in the family that had a stable income during the pandemic.

Like many cities in Cook County, Skokie had slowly begun to reopen. After successfully completing a previously planned construction project, the Skokie Public Library reopened and became available to the public in June 2021.

During our interview, Baig sat in an enclosed study room in the library. He alternated between fidgeting with his pencil and holding his phone. As the interview progressed, he gradually relaxed and sat farther back in his chair. He allowed light laughter to decorate the ends of his sentences and opened up more about his experiences during the COVID-19 pandemic.

I HAD COVID pretty much a week after the limited overtime we got at my work. Probably got it at work. For the first few days, I was really sick, like I hadn't been this sick in years, so I definitely knew this is something new. I just remember this really high fever. I had a bunch of symptoms that I looked up. It was kind of tricky to diagnose just by symptoms, but I did go ahead and get tested, and I was positive.

I would say, three days I was really sick, fourth day I was getting better, fifth day I was pretty much back to normal. I would just be in my room, and I would keep everybody out of it. My mom would try to come in and give me food, but I was telling her to leave it and then leave the room and just keep it as short as possible, so that way she doesn't contract any of it. She's taking these thyroid meds that suppress the immune system; it's really not good. Like, if she catches it and she's already had asthma... I was way more concerned because this is not something I've ever experienced before.

I started working at the end of February [2020], right when the pandemic kind of blew up. [I make] slightly over minimum wage. I usually got to close, which means I'm coming in some time in the afternoon and then pretty much staying there until 10 p.m., pretty much the whole day on the weekends. Most of the job is just stocking the shelves and making sure customers can find whatever they come in looking for. But as a shift leader, I got to do that in addition to counting the safe every night, making the deposit, and a few other extra duties.

A lot of stuff changed because of the pandemic. There are people who don't feel comfortable working there anymore, so you're naturally understaffed, but at the same time, people are trying to come in and stock up on everything. The grocery stores were pretty much the busiest, and people will be, like, fighting over toilet paper and cough syrup and stuff like that.

We had to put limits on these items so people couldn't buy as many, but they would still work their way around it. We limited them per transaction, but people would have multiple transactions and take as many as they needed. It was, like, a fake shortage almost. People thought [toilet paper] was going to run out, and then they started buying more, and then they actually were starting to run out.

It was really stressful and draining to work with the bare minimum of [staff]. It takes a lot of time to get next to nothing.

[The staffing shortage] was kind of a blessing and a curse. I was like, "Since I'm going in there already three days a week, I might as well go in five." They also were promising unlimited overtime, and that sounded really good, especially considering my school was closed and everything. This was a good opportunity to have some extra cash because you never know what might happen.

I'm only working weekends now instead of four or five days a week. Sometimes I'll even call off those days, like if I need to put in more work for school, like if it's midterms week or finals week. I feel like it's way easier to manage, even though I have extra classes, more classes than I've ever taken, this semester. I feel like [school] is way easier to manage because in-person classes are just so much easier than online classes.

If in the future something like COVID happens again and I'm working as a programmer or something, I'll be able to still have my job because I can do my work remotely. Your employment is kind of certain in that sense. You don't have to come into contact with anybody too. It's really much more flexible than a lot of other professions. Best part is you get a lot of money. It's not a Walgreens shift leader.

Everybody in my house had a job, but ever since the pandemic hit, literally nobody had a job except me and my mom. She babysits at somebody's place. Since I'm one of the only ones working, I feel like there is definitely more pressure on me. When I started chipping in more, it kind of put into perspective how much everything costs.

There's no way I'd be able to actually just pay rent and get my groceries and stuff off [a job] like this. Ever since [the pandemic began], it really made me prioritize my education over work. Previously, I would want to work as much as I could and try to just rush my homework with the time that I left.

It's pretty pointless trying to work at one of these jobs. By "these" I mean minimum wage jobs, because the amount of money that you get for your time, you could just take that time instead and invest it in yourself. [Learning] a new skill or something is basically like an investment. There will be more you can do and there will be more you can earn with what you're doing.

— NOELLE ROSA

I'm just anxious to see [my boys], because now I have time. I'm off, and now I have time to travel to see them.

Do You Ever Get to Be Treated like a Human?

ESTHER CLARK, RETIREE

Esther Clark's kindhearted resilience could be heard through her voice even before she managed to turn on her camera. This Zoom interview took place in early February 2021, a few months after her retirement. She sat with a smile in a room with yellow wallpaper.

Clark has two incarcerated family members, a son and a nephew. She calls them both her "boys" because they grew up together. They were incarcerated as teens in the 1990s for a homicide. Twenty-five years later, they were still in prison when the COVID-19 pandemic began.

MY NAME IS Esther Clark.

I have a son and a nephew who are currently in the Department of Corrections. My nephew was 15 and my son was 17 when the incident happened. They've been in prison for twenty-five years. They got in when they were teenagers, so they got a chance to get that resentencing, but to me, they still gave them hard sentences. I believe they have over-served their time. It's time for them to get out and do something good with their lives.

[My son] is the apple of my eye. He's a very smart, bright young man, and it just seems like he got thrown in an animal cage and forgot about. But he is very smart. He reads a lot. He goes to school. He works in the kitchen. While he works in the kitchen, he also got COVID.

He's recently got over the COVID-19. He's back to work, and he told me now they're going to call him an essential worker because he's been walking around, taking trays, doing what he has to do, which is good for him, but my youngest son, my nephew—I call him my son because they were raised together—he was the youngest, but he got the most time because he was deemed the shooter.

He's been going to school in there, but when they got the COVID in Galesburg,[97] they shut down all their schooling.

---

[97] Hill Correctional Facility in Galesburg, Illinois, is a medium-security prison that in 2021 housed 1,577 inmates. Source: https://www2.illinois.gov/idoc/facilities/Pages/hillcorrectionalcenter.aspx

He's still helped clean the place. He's a very nice guy. He just got caught up with the wrong people. Kids that like to be busy, that like to be doing something, they're bored, and in the environment that we came from on the West Side, it was just a zoo. Survival of the fittest. To say this group is over here, that group is over there, and they rivals—it just escalates, escalates, escalates.

He goes to school when he can, trying to stay in class, trying to learn stuff. He's always in the law library. I told him, "When you come home, boy, you have to be a lawyer." He's always reading the law, criminal law. He's telling me about how it goes.

They're keeping clean records, which is not easy in prison. You get tickets[98] for little to nothing. And they have been keeping low profiles and just doing what they got to do to make time go by so they can get out. That's time that I cannot wait, because I miss [them] so much.

· · · · · · ·
· · · · · · · · · · · ·
· · · · · · · · ·

With COVID-19, it gets complicated. That's what makes it hard. Now it's been almost a year since I had any right to go see them. I try to go see them when I can, but I got two of them, so it makes it awkward because last year I was working, see? I just retired in May [2020], so I would set up traveling to see one and then go to see the other one.

Before COVID-19, it was a little better, except it was like you were being held hostage too, going to the prisons, because they have so many strict rules that just going to the jailhouse is crazy. The way they search you, some of them, the way they talk to you—it's just horrible.

I would take vacation and go back and forth, but it would be awkward because sometimes you make plans. I'll call down there, and they'll say, "Oh, well, we're on lockdown." I say, "Do you know when you'll be off lockdown?" They say, "No, you have to call back to find out."

There's all kind of obstacles. Even when you get there, if your clothing isn't right, or if your pants are too tight, or if your shirt dips below your neck, they'll find all kind of things to deter you from coming. You can't wear rings, you can't wear earrings, you can't wear necklaces. At different prisons, you don't know what you might run into going back and forth.

I learned my lessons: how to dress, what to do. Have an open mind and be ready for anything, because you never know who had a bad day. They might be taking it out on you. I've seen a lot of that. There's a lot of people ahead of me in line, and you see something happen, and you ask, "Do I got that right," or, "Do I have this paper?"

---

[98] Disciplinary infractions can earn inmates tickets that may count against them if they apply for early release. Source: https://prisonprofessors.com/disciplinary-actions/

You know what the most troubling part is? They jack up the money on the food. When I go down to see them, I will take my cousin or someone with me so we can bring both [my son and my nephew] out at the same time, because they put us in separate places. You can't talk to them [together]. You can only talk to the person that you're there with. So, I visit [my son] one day, and then [my nephew] the other day.

I'm just anxious to see [my boys], because now I have time. I'm off, and now I have time to travel to see them. But with lockdown, you don't know what to think about or what to expect. Both have had COVID-19 since they been in there. They both have. That's scary.

I get to talk to them on the phone, but [the prisons] cut their phone time back. Before we had half an hour. Now it's fifteen minutes. They would come out [of their cells] every two days, I think.

Now it's getting better. My nephew is able to call me every day now, because they let them out ninety minutes a day. But my son, with him working, he is out off and on anyways, so he gets a chance to call me. It's getting better as COVID-19 [cases go] down.

Most of the time, we talk about getting out. What's going on with their cases? How's everybody in the family? Is everyone good? They can't wait for the first time they have a visit so I can come. Just mostly family things. You know, family and people, because you know how it is when you're away from family. You want to know how everybody is.

•••••• •••••
•••••••• •••

They were real upset at first [when the pandemic started], because [the guards] don't tell them at all what's going on. They just move them. They just move them around out of their areas, but they don't tell them that it's COVID-19 or who has it. They just start moving people around.

When [my son] was in there by himself, he figured what's going on. And it's upsetting to watch it. Then they moved my nephew out somewhere else, and he found out that everyone in there had COVID, and he's like, "I don't have it. I'm trying to get away from that, so don't put me in here. Test me again." He said they have started doing testing pretty good. I said, "Well, that's good."

COVID has affected a lot of people. It's just bad.

The other thing they were saying was the guards, they can go around and talk and hug and do what they want to do, but for [the prisoners], they can't not have their masks on. But the guards can go around without their masks on, talking. When really, they're the ones that's bringing it in. 'Cause [my boys have] been there for two, three years. How are they going to bring it in? The guards are the ones that need to get tested.

So, finally, they started testing the guards. So that's a beautiful thing, 'cause at least you know where it's coming from. Except that once they find out a guard has something, they have to test them all or quarantine them [the prisoners], which is crazy.

So the biggest complaint is that the guards are not being held accountable. They going around, not wearing masks, and they should be reprimanded. Everybody should wear the mask. They were right about that. That was their biggest complaint, that the guards were getting away with stuff, and then [the prisoners] get a ticket if they don't wear masks. But the guards talk, huddle, play.

• • • • • • • •
• • • • • • • • • • •
• • • • • • • • •

[One day] my nephew's like, "I'm scared for you out there, especially with all these carjackings and stuff." I see they're coming after Jeeps, and I have a Grand Cherokee. "Just give it some gas and go." I'm like, yeah. We talked about all of that. The different murders of innocent people. Everything. The new president, the old president.

[My boys] couldn't believe that they stormed the Capitol. I said, "Son, my mouth is open too." I am shocked. I've never ever heard of anything like that before. Even when you go to DC, or you go to the Capitol, you're not going anywhere you're not supposed to be, doing anything you're not supposed to be. I'm just appalled, appalled that people got away with that. All my years of voting, being a registered voter, I've never heard of anything like that before.

[Trump] is going to tell that big lie that they stole the election from him, and they believe it. How? You hear a lot of stuff, but that's the craziest ever. I've never heard of that before, man. When people stormed in the Capitol building, I was looking at it with my mouth open. I ain't never seen anything like that before. And why you don't have guards? Why you don't have the National Guard there? And they already told you that these people is coming. As soon as they [Trump supporters] came down there, it's like the floodgates were open to "Come on, do whatever you want to do. We know you're coming to do something. You're OK. You're white, so you're right." That's wrong. That's just messed up.

People know money speaks. Money. If you got money and you can buy one of those high-priced lawyers, they're going to get in there and they're going to do it for you. And [my boys] know that too. If I could have afforded one of those high-priced lawyers, they wouldn't have had that much time. They look at it like it is, a double standard. They already knew that.

Most of the people in prison are Black, and they have them in rural white areas, so can you imagine what they face on a daily basis? So, my nephew is really into that one [racial inequities in sentencing]. He's like, "Do you know how these people treat us in here?" I'm like, "Nah, but I can imagine." And he said, "Whatever you imagine times ten." And I said, "Yeah, 'cause I see how they treat us when we come down there."

Sometimes there's a nice guy that says, "You can't wear your rings" [during a visit] instead of making you go all the way back. Can't do this, can't do that, whatever. And then you got some that you can just tell don't like you. You know how you get that feeling when someone doesn't like you? That's for real. Just sense them people don't like you.

They run into that a lot. They said, "Mama, you just got to try to keep your mouth shut. They talk to us like we're two years old, but we're grown men."

That's the other thing; they don't have any respect for them for being human.

My nephew wrote me this little thing, saying that all they got to do is just treat you like you're human. That's all. True, they did wrong things. They know they did wrong things—they accepted that, and they put in a lot of time. So what do you want from them? Blood? What do you want?

They were teenagers when they went to jail. They didn't know anything. They were just running out there being wild, doing what they do, and got caught up. OK, so now you took twenty-five years off their life. If you don't learn something in ten years from being in a cage, when are you going to learn? Do you ever get to be treated like a human? He said being in there, you never get treated like a human, [you get] treated like a monkey or something, and they talk to you any kind of way. These are grown men, and they don't like that. And you can't blame them.

They've been confined in the zoo, and they want out. We just want out. They want to see what it feels like to get up, wash your face, and look out a window.

The reason I can speak on that is because I have a cousin who recently got out of prison. He had been in there for nine years. But he had been in and out before that. After the nine years, he said all he longed for is to have somewhere where he can feel comfortable and safe because you don't sleep well while in prison. You don't eat well while in prison. You don't do nothing but try to watch your back.

He came over here and spent a few nights with me. He said, "When I go in that room, and I close that door, I know that no one's going to open that door." Can you imagine? He said he slept like a log. So, yeah, I think that after you spent so many years in there, you have to be rehabilitated or something.

If you don't have anything, if you don't have college, at least have a little trade school so that when they come out, they know how to do something with themselves. The problem is you lock them away, and they have nothing to do. So when they come out, they just get out and do the same stupid thing they were doing before. And that's just messed up, just messed up.

[My boy] believes in helping the other inmates train themselves. He said, "Mama, can you believe some guys in here can't read? They don't have anybody on the outside. It is sort of rough in here, and you got to mingle 'cause you in here with them." And I said, "Yeah, well, you're like one of those good guys. You have a giving heart like your mama." So, he gives them a shirt when they come in here with nothing.

We let him do the correspondence classes, and that's good, but my nephew, now he's stuck because, with COVID-19, you can't go to class. They can't do anything. So now I'm going to have to find him some kind of correspondence class to show them that he's doing something with himself, something positive.

It's hard because you want the best for your kids. You want to see them progress in whatever way they can, but with this [COVID-19], it's like they just shut him in a cage and threw the key away and tell the ringmasters to have at them.

I'll tell you; I've been in prison. I've been in prison for twenty-five years. That's what it feels like. You put people in one heck of a situation. You know, like solitary. Torture. My nephew tells me that the cell they are in, you can reach out and touch both walls. Some people can mentally handle it, but some people get scared.

They need to find a way to rehabilitate them because a lot of these people have been exposed to nothing in life.

—JOHN GIESA

A Day of Rest

COREY BROOKS, PASTOR

As the leader and founder of New Beginnings Church in Chicago's Woodlawn neighborhood on the South Side, Pastor Corey Brooks has been working for the past twenty years to reduce violence in his congregants' neighborhoods and draw new members into New Beginnings' fold.

Brooks also runs the not-for-profit Project H.O.O.D., or Helping Others Obtain Destiny. The organization is dedicated to providing the tools necessary for individuals to become peacemakers, leaders, and entrepreneurs within their own communities. "We seek to equip," their creed reads, "not to excuse."[99] The central cog that holds these many-wheeled machines together, Brooks—along with his dedicated team—serves as a faith leader, a community organizer, and a friend.

During our conversation, he acknowledged the toll that 2020 has taken on him mentally, spiritually, and emotionally. The COVID-19 pandemic rendered in-person religious services impossible, and without the opportunity to physically connect with his members, Brooks and his fellow pastors had to get creative. They found innovative ways to bridge the gaps borne out of social distancing and even established some new outreach and service traditions.

When speaking of his plans, Brooks referred to the work behind these initiatives with a collective "we," careful to acknowledge the individuals who share his passion for healing and nurturing the people they serve.

Brooks was warm and wise, with a glass-half-full mentality. His earnestness emanated through the Zoom call as we spoke on a sunny day in February 2021.

MY MOM SENT ME a text message. She's dealing with cancer.

It said, "I wish someone had told me what I'm getting ready to tell you." And I thought, *OK, what's going on?*

She said, "Corey, God has been too good to you for you not to be good to yourself."

And then I said, "What do you mean?"

---

99 Source: https://www.projecthood.org/

She said, "Well, you need to take care of yourself mentally. You need to take care of yourself physically and take care of yourself spiritually."

And I thought she was right. I have not done a great job in 2020 of taking care of myself mentally. I have not done a great job taking care of myself physically, and I have not done a great job taking care of myself spiritually.

I know biblically you want to take a day of rest. I know it mentally, I know it biblically, but realistically doing it is where I have the problem.

My daughter, who is 25 and really sharp, is planning to *make* me take a break. She wants us to go to Colombia. I have a mentor that is giving her a financial gift to make me go on a trip. And I haven't taken vacations in two or three years. So that's the type of stuff I'm going to do better. I would just like to go out on a boat and just chill and enjoy the people and markets. And I'm really interested in the fact that a lot of Africans were let off in Colombia. I'm interested in seeing that mixture of some of the cultures.

Until then, I'm just going to take a little small break. A day here or an hour there.

The fact that I've always wanted to help a lot of people keeps me like just going, going, going, going, but I realize, I *know* I need a break. But failure for the community is a bigger deal for me.

. . . .
. . . .
. . . .

Mentally, this is probably—and I haven't shared this, so I'm sharing it now—mentally, last year was probably my toughest year because there were so many people in need. We had so many people who were getting sick, and we were having to try to do funerals for people and trying to keep everybody together.

We send out text messages, we send out calls, ask our members: "Do you need anything? You need food, or you need this?" And we assist all of our members to make sure everybody's need is met. So it's all about us trying to meet needs during the pandemic.

We did some outside stuff at first, and when it started getting really bad according to news reports and stuff, we started saying, "OK, we're just going to focus on feeding people." And those became like our big events. If you go back and look at our summer feeding, it will amaze you the videos from it, all the people that we were able to serve. That kind of helped offset some of that fellowship that we were missing, because it gave our church members opportunity to come out to serve and be around people. For instance, I can remember our sanctuary was full of about fifty women from our church or fifty men from our church, packing vegetables. We've been feeding at least five thousand families every month last year since June.

June, July, August, September, we did these feedings. You can find it on social media. We recorded it. We had cars, lines for at least a mile long. Then we had all of these organizations that helped us, like the Cubs, who would buy all these vegetables and things like that. Ozinga Concrete, Oberweis ice cream, Metro Ford. All these people helped us to buy food. We really focused on feeding people because we live in such a food desert.[100]

The other thing that's been really tough during this pandemic is just how we do ministry. We have to really use social media: Facebook, Instagram, Twitter. We're using this stuff more than ever, and we've really enhanced our media ministry to do that as well. There's broadband difficulties, and it's very unfortunate because you would think in America, everybody should have Wi-Fi and broadband services. But that's not true in the inner city. I'm thinking if it's like that in the inner cities, I can just imagine how it must be in some rural areas.

And we do drive-bys. I have a couple people that will go by some of our elderly. They don't have a family, or they haven't been able to come to church. We'll go by, especially when it's warmer during the summer and when they're behind the door to talk to them, just interact. And we'll do that again coming up, starting in March, as it begins to warm up until this pandemic is over. But really caring for our elderly in our community, especially ones who are members of our church—we're really trying to make sure that we do that.

Some people just don't want to do church. They don't want anything to do with church. But we still need to reach people, we still need to help people.

We created Project H.O.O.D. for that very reason, to fight violence and to fight poverty. One of the things I'm really proud about that we did—our church and Project H.O.O.D., when the pandemic was happening and when the riots were happening—is that some of the drug stores and pharmacies were looted and they weren't open in our neighborhoods. So we organized to take our seniors to go get their medicine in suburban areas. When a lady called us and said, "Hey, I'm on dialysis and I can't get my medicine because the pharmacy has been looted. I need to get my medicine, Pastor." To organize her being able to go pick that medicine up at a suburban Walgreens was a blessing.

Another is our violence prevention program. We have about twelve employees that work violence prevention. Their sole purpose is to make sure that we eliminate violence in our neighborhood and really get a handle on the gun violence and the gangs.

---

[100] A food desert is an area with limited access to affordable and nutritious food, especially predominant in lower-income neighborhoods and communities. Source: "Food, Conservation, and Energy Act of 2008, 110th Cong, 2nd Sess, HR 6124, Title VII," http://www.gpo.gov/fdsys/pkg/BILLS-110hr6124eh/pdf/BILLS-110hr6124eh.pdf

Our violence prevention team has been working harder during the pandemic than they were working before the pandemic, making sure that they get involved in the community as much as possible, finding out who's doing what as much as possible. They've had to make some serious adjustments to get on top of the gun violence. They've done a great job, because when you look at the gun violence in Chicago and all around us, in our area, it's [started to go back] down, which is amazing.

They're going out into the neighborhood, into the areas where there have been problems, and they're passing out PPE [to people] and making conversations with people in the community, letting them know that we've got a violence prevention hotline, things like that. They're just doing the best they can.

Thus far, thankfully, none of them have gotten COVID or anything. We try to use all the social-distance measures possible.

Twenty years ago, we started New Beginnings Church, and our whole focus was reaching people who were, at that time I used to say "ridiculed, resisted, and rejected."

We're a non-denominational church. We're a Christian evangelical church, though, if that makes sense. We are an evangelical church, but we just don't participate in a denomination.

It's hard, you know, especially when your whole identity is built around fellowship. I mean, when we talk about Black church, that's what we do. Getting together, spending time together, fellowship. That's our church life.

And to take that apart, take that away, has been difficult. Personally, it's probably been one of the toughest times as a pastor. Not so much because I'm not still preaching, because we still preach every Sunday. But I'm a people person—I'm a straight extrovert. I love people. I love being around people. And [to] take that away is like, whoa.

I think our people, our culture—not just our African American culture, but our church culture—we base our church on being a hugging, lovey, loving church. I don't see that leaving our church. I think once we start getting people vaccinated, we'll be right back to the way it used to be.

Our goal is to start [in-person services] the first Sunday in July [2021]. By that time, we hope that a lot of our members would have had the vaccine. I mean, at our church, we do COVID testing [for the community] every day. And now starting Saturday, we're going to start providing the vaccine shots. We should be able to help a lot of people in our community with the COVID testing and the vaccine shot, and we're working in conjunction with Howard Brown Health Facility.[101] So that's a big, big thing.

We've been growing. We have some new members and people who are part of our membership now. We're going to work even harder to get more new members. We were just planning our summer program yesterday, so we're really excited about what we're going to do.

On Friday nights, we're going to do some type of music for seniors in our neighborhood. We figured since everybody's been cooped up, this would be a good opportunity for seniors to come outside. We'll do some salsa or line dancing and all that. We'll pick them up in vans, bring them and drop them off back at home, and we'll have healthy food for them to try out.

Then on Saturday, underneath that same tent, we're going to transform it to a farmer's market to promote healthy food options. And then we're going to still pass out our food like we normally do.

On Saturday night, we're going to turn that into a thing for kids to be able to watch movies, like a movie night, and we'll have healthy food options again. And then on Sunday, since we haven't been able to have church, we're going to have church outside all summer long underneath that tent.

Late Sunday afternoon going into Sunday night, we're going to have some contemporary gospel concerts. And we'll use that to hopefully get new members, introduce people to the church, introduce people to healthy food options, help people emotionally because they're going to be able to fellowship and get together. Everything we're going to do, we're gonna stream it and show other churches, "Hey, you could do this. You can do some of these same things."

I want to go help people do what we've done in this city. I don't want to run their stuff, I just want to come alongside and become a mentor and coach. That would be a dream come true. So, start with Chicago and hopefully we can move to America, and then hopefully we move to the world.

— EMILY RICHARDS

---

[101] Howard Brown Health provides LGBTQ populations with affordable healthcare. Source: https://howardbrown.org/about/

He gestured energetically as he spoke,
and when he reached a difficult memory,
his legs became restless.

A Little Bit of Kindness

AARON SMITH, BARISTA

Twenty-year-old Aaron Smith has spent the last few years living with his mother and sister in their La Grange apartment, though it has never been home. His mother has long been prone to bouts of physical and verbal abuse. Smith described in sad bewilderment how she has even blamed him for the division of their family.

After an altercation with his sister over his mother's abuse, Smith was taken into custody by police. He soon found himself in holding alongside men who, to him, seemed all too comfortable in a cell. He was released, but he was not allowed to return to his apartment while the legal case was settled. Instead, he temporarily went to stay with his aunt just as COVID-19 hit. He is now living with his mother and sister again.

Despite the sometimes grim nature of his story, Smith tried to laugh through it. He gestured energetically as he spoke, and when he reached a difficult memory, his legs became restless. During the interview, he eagerly showed me his living space, though he was anxious to leave before his mother returned from work.

MY MOM DID NOT WANT a boy. I was told by people in my family that my mom literally cried—not tears of joy—when she found out I was a boy. When my mom left my dad, he was in a position financially where he couldn't take us. So my mom kind of just took us and then left, and I had no say in it. I had nowhere else to go.

My entire support system was fourteen hours away in Washington, DC, and I was with my abusive mother and my sister, who couldn't care less about how my mom treated me. Maybe she didn't want to deal with what I was going through. If she intervened, she'd probably be going through the same stuff.

When I was in high school, I tried reporting it to my school. This is when she would physically abuse me a lot, and I was still a little younger, like 16, so I couldn't really do much about it.

They had an investigation, and she lied about the whole situation. She said that I lied to them because I was angry that she took my phone away, which didn't even happen. They believed her for some reason, and it was dropped.

And then I got more shit from my mom for that. So I was put into a position where I'm trying to help myself, [but] I can't leave.

•••••• •
•••••••••• •••
•••••••••

Not only could I not get a job because I had this shit on my record, I couldn't get a job because everything was shut down. No one was hiring. Everyone—the world—was freaking out because of COVID.

Me and my girlfriend, Andrea, had to be quarantined together because she was over when everything was happening. We were in my aunt's house for weeks, dude. And I was so depressed, I didn't do anything. I slept on a mattress on the floor. I didn't have a job; I couldn't pay for a bed.

After COVID, I dropped out of community college, I was so depressed. I didn't want to do online classes. I was just existing at that point. My uncle got me in at a job. I thought I'd be working at Costco, like I'd have the vest on, be welcoming people in. You know, like, "Can I see that receipt, sir?" That's what I thought I would be doing.

He lied. It wasn't at Costco. I guess that's my fault for not really looking into the fine print of everything. I worked the horrible-ass night shift, 10 p.m. till 10 a.m. I would drive like an hour to Morris, Illinois, every day in my already-shit car.

Instead of stocking stuff, like a normal, Walmart-type beat, I had a yellow-ass jumpsuit. I had a fucking hose, dude. They had me working as a sanitation person for the meat production facility. I was scrubbing down the conveyor belt, breaking down machines, power hosing. I was like, are you kidding me, dude? I'm 18 doing this shit? This is someone who failed at life. I should not be here.

There [was] nobody around my age. A lot of them had kids. You know, I just couldn't relate to them. I didn't really get to know any of them. I just went there, made my money. It was horrible. All I did was wake up, go to work, come home, eat, maybe take a shower if I had the energy for it, go to sleep, wake up at 7 p.m. I had no social life, I didn't do anything. I was just really, really depressed.

For the first few days, I had someone showing me around, and I thought that I'd be working with a partner the whole time. It made it bearable that I had somebody else to work with.

My third week, they threw me in a room by myself, and I had to clean the whole thing. That's when I walked out. I was like, I'm not doing this. And on my way home, I called Andrea. I literally wanted to cry.

It was like two in the morning, I was listening to music, and I had a moment where there was something telling me, really telling me, that I should go a hundred on this highway and shift into the next lane and just end my shit right there.

After I quit, my aunt screamed at me and then cut me off. I guess she was disappointed that I wasn't doing anything. I had to kiss my mom's ass just to come back; I basically admitted to my mom that everything she did to me was fine, and it was OK for her to treat me like this, and that I was in the wrong, just so I can have a place to stay.

And even while doing that, she didn't give me house keys. I would have to sleep in my car or somewhere else because I couldn't go into the house. When the door was locked, I would tell maintenance people, "Oh, yeah, I went out to get some groceries. I was half awake. Can you guys unlock the door? I won't do it again." I acted my ass off.

· · · · · · · · · · · · · ·
· · · · · · · · · · · ·

I applied to Starbucks by my house. Applied off a whim. No previous experience. I didn't even list that [other] job. They were hiring everyone, and I just happened to get hired.

Whenever I'd come home from work, I would shower, try to be clean whenever I could. Sometimes I would have to stay in my car because [my mom] wouldn't let me in the house past nine, even though I would get off work at 9:30, sometimes twelve.

I was at Starbucks basically all day. I was like, "Who wants shifts taken? I can take shifts; I can work a double." So I was usually working twelve-, thirteen-hour shifts. I felt a lot happier there. I even told my boss, "Yeah, I would rather be at Starbucks than at my house right now."

It wasn't as bad as it sounds because I was making money, and I had stuff to keep me busy. I was at Starbucks from open to close, and it didn't feel bad at the time. Now, I'm like, I did my time already. I'm not struggling no more; I don't need to work no doubles.

I wasn't really deterred by the fact that I was up for fourteen hours on my feet, and then I did it again the next day. I was tired, you know, but I wouldn't complain. I was happy to be there because really, it was so much better than the alternative. And it's so crazy that I'm saying that like it's a normal thing. That should not be normal.

I just wanted more for myself, you know? I didn't want to be content with the life that I was living. I was like, *Is this really all there is for me?* I had a really shit hand dealt to me; I didn't want that to be the legacy that I left. I wanted to stick it to people who have their whole life handed to them and they do nothing with it, where people like me have to work for basically everything.

I got nothing handed to me. My car was a gift, that was the one thing that I didn't have to work for. And the only reason I had that car is because a family friend from the Philippines was not here legally, and ICE[102] was looking for her. She had to go back before she was going to get deported, so she sold me her car for five hundred. It was really sad, but it was also a blessing.

If I did not have that car, I would probably be dead in a ditch somewhere. I would have nowhere to sleep. That car, that's my freedom right there. That was my wings, you know? I could go anywhere.

• • • • • • •
• • • • • • • • • • •
• • • • • • • • •

During peak COVID, we didn't have any chairs in the café. It was like, you get your drink, you go. Put your mask on or we're going to yell at you. We have masks to give to people.

[Customers would come in] like, "Oh, I forgot my mask."

"Oh, we have one for you," or whatever.

This guy came in. He didn't want to wear a mask, refused to wear a mask. And we were like, "Sir. If you want to be in the store, we require you to wear a mask."

He's like, "Fine. I'll take your stupid mask."

So he took a mask just to run over to the trash to throw it out. And then he went back and got another one and just kept doing that.

We're like, "Dude, this is the third mask we've given you. Wear it or get out."

And he was like, "Well, I don't fucking want to be here anyways."

What is the point? You're protesting at a Starbucks, really? You're doing this in front of a bunch of teenagers who are just here to work for college or support themselves? Like, we don't care. Literally just be considerate of other people, please.

I couldn't afford to get COVID, so I was really anal about the whole thing. I was like, bro, please put your mask on, because if I get sick, then I'm done, you know? I was living out my car, and I have asthma as well, so I didn't want to get sick.

During the peak of the coronavirus, there was a rumor that started that corona doesn't affect Black people, and there were fake statistics to back that. So I was really going into that, like, I don't give a fuck, this doesn't affect me. I'm half Black, why do I care? And then my aunt got COVID, and I was like, I don't know if I can believe this rumor anymore; this is too close to me, bro.

---

102 Immigration and Customs Enforcement. Source: https://www.ice.gov/

It's just crazy that was a rumor. And a lot of people, including myself, believed that at first. It's so racially motivated. Of course they said that, so Black people walk unmasked and catch corona.

· · · · · · · ·
: : : : : : : : · · · ·
· · · · · · · · ·

I like my job. That's the one thing that saved me during the whole pandemic. I feel like my coworkers I don't even see as coworkers. I haven't worked that many jobs, so I had the idea that people don't get that close to their coworkers. I don't walk into a McDonald's and have them know me by my name or by my order.

Almost everyone in our store knows the majority of the customers' names, order, and even random shit about them. Like, oh, this person is a yoga instructor, or this person's a science teacher, or this person does real estate.

And the coworkers are super supportive as well. When I legit lived out of my car for almost three months, they were super supportive about that. No one was making fun of me for wearing the same clothes or smelling bad or anything.

And they were giving me resources. My one coworker, Jalen, was like, "I can help you come up with a plan to build your credit and manage it, so you can get a new car." It was super helpful. I'm like, wow, you guys literally went out of your way to just talk to me or do this shit for me.

I really worked my ass off at that job. I never called off. I worked almost forty hours a week when I first started. My hours are more chill now because I'm more financially stable. I don't want to say 100 percent, but I have income coming in so I can spend stuff and not feel like I'm stressing, you know? I'm paying for my own phone.

Just being in that positive environment gave me the energy to work on myself and figure out who I wanted to be in life. It's a job that I never thought I would work, and it wasn't anything like I thought it was going to be. It was really fun making drinks and connecting and talking to people, getting to know my regulars and being a positive influence on some people's lives, you know?

There's literally a review, if you look up the downtown La Grange Starbucks, where someone's like, "I had a really, really shit day today, but the barista at Starbucks talked to me and made me feel a lot better about everything." And I'm pretty sure I talked to that person, so that really made me feel good.

You just don't know what people are going through. You could be sitting right next to a person who could be having the worst day in their life, and you'd never know.

There's not a lot of compassion in this world. I feel like if everyone was a little bit kinder, if everyone just cared a little bit more, the world would be a better place.

—ELLE EVANS

As the interview began, Salamanca was smiling and relaxing in his chair, eager to talk.

Don't Watch the News

CELSO SALAMANCA, INVENTORY CONTROL MANAGER

Celso Salamanca is an inventory control manager at Home Products International in the West Elsdon neighborhood of Chicago. Originally from Mexico City, Salamanca moved to the Chicago area in 1994. He attended school for some time, then worked part time at a local restaurant. Later, he found his first professional role with Home Products. Salamanca has now been with HPI for twenty-six years.

This interview was conducted right after the daily ping-pong tournament that HPI employees partake in during lunch in October 2021. Salamanca happens to be the reigning champion. As the interview began, Salamanca was smiling and relaxing in his chair, eager to talk.

I REMEMBER FIRST HEARING about COVID-19 when I was at the China Buffet with my wife. We were there when the news was talking about [COVID-19] in China, where it started. I told my wife, "Nah, this is not going to come to the United States," because we are, kind of—how do you call it? One of the countries that are on top of everything, right? So I said, "Nah, it's not coming here," and then suddenly, boom, it hit us! I thought it was just going to be a month or two, whatever. Obviously, I was wrong about that.

My role at HPI is inventory control manager, so every morning I get sent two reports, the negative-inventory report and the machine-timing report. The negative-inventory report tells me which products we have negative inventory in, and then I can focus on getting those products made so we can ship them to the retailers. The machine-timing report tells me how good the machines are running so I can plan how long it will take us to make those products.

I really like coming to work because I know what to do, and it's not like people are on top of you. Everyone here knows that I know what I'm doing, you know? Everyone trusts me here. I'm the kind of person that talks to everyone and is friendly, you know? So that's what I like about HPI.

For work, we never stopped running, right? But the pandemic changed HPI because the simple things like going to lunch and having all these people around you [were] no longer a thing. Suddenly, we would go to lunch, but everyone is divided and you feel like you're in jail, you know? "Hey, I'll sell you a cigarette, but pass me a tortilla, whatever."

As far as my job and for the company, you know, everything stopped coming in. We got short on all the machine parts, like rows or wheels. All of that comes from China, and they were not producing it, and we couldn't get it anyways because there was also no shipping. On that part, the pandemic hit us economically.

In the plant, a lot of the workers were kind of scared of people. Some people didn't take it as seriously as other people. But we had to kind of clean everything and social distance and everything.

At the beginning of the pandemic, there was no such thing as having a birthday party, even with close family. We didn't celebrate nothing at all.

As of right now, people are kind of starting to get back [to normal]. With the vaccine right now, it's getting better. We feel more secure because we already know that when we do celebrate parties or Mother's Day or whatever, all the ones around you got the shot, the vaccine.

But people are still a little scared. People still don't believe in the COVID vaccine. I say, millions of people already took the vaccine. Some people think the government wants to kill people, [but] that's not what happened. I mean, I have family that say, "If God is telling me that it is my time to leave, then it's time for me to leave." I tell them that's not the case, because God said, "I do my part, you do your part." So [God] already gave the knowledge for the vaccine, so now you have to do your part and take the vaccine.

· · · · · · · ·
· · · · · · · · · · · ·
· · · · · · · · · ·

During quarantine, I just stayed at home watching TV and the news. No visiting and no nothing. But watching TV and the news was the one of the major things that made people get desperate because it just showed people getting sicker. They were repeating the same thing every day, every day, every day, and you get sick of that. I got sick of that. So I stopped watching TV. I turned it off for good. When I stopped watching the news, I was less nervous and more calm, because I wasn't thinking about that. Even though you know it's there, you're not thinking of that all the time. Just go do something else than just thinking about all these negative things you see on TV.

I'm hearing from a lot of people that they did the same thing. You know people are thinking, "Is that true or is that not really true?" I see on Facebook things like, "I came to this place where they said there were trailers full of sick people and I'm here, but I don't see nothing here." That's where you start to think, *Is that really happening?* So that's why I say, you know what? Forget about it. A lot of people are saying the same thing: Just don't watch the news.

You know what I started noticing? You never hear good news. It's always bad news. So where is the good news? Like someone saving someone's life or whatever, but no, it's all bad news. Especially here in Chicago, it's always some shooting, carjacking, COVID death, or whatever. The TV and the news always throw at you what they want you to know, not good things. It just makes things around here seem bad because they never say, "Something good happened around here."

I even remember seeing on the news a long time ago—it was in Spain or some other distant country—and they were putting masks on the dogs. I'm picturing telling my granddaughters, "Hey, on this day, it was a bad pandemic, we had to wear masks, couldn't visit any family, and they were even putting masks on dogs."[103]

Now that things are slowly improving, I'm paying more attention to the news because I know it's not that bad as it was in the beginning. I pay attention, but I don't really worry about it.

— DAVID ROUBALIK

---

[103] There was at least one report early in the pandemic that some pet owners in China were putting masks on their dogs as a precaution against COVID-19. Source: https://www.insider.com/coronavirus-face-masks-pets-dogs-2020-3#face-masks-also-dont-help-prevent-the-spread-of-the-virus-4

Vaughan herself is a bright, colorful, smiley, intelligent, passionate woman of color.

Looking For Light

NIKA VAUGHAN, SHOP OWNER

Nika Vaughan is the owner of Plant Salon in Chicago's West Town area, encompassing the neighborhoods of Wicker Park and Noble Square, among others. She opened the business during the pandemic as a means to increase income while her other company, Nika Vaughan Bridal Artist, lost revenue.

Plant Salon is a place quiet in terms of noise but loud in life and color, with the sound of soulful music playing. The plants of the shop are arranged the same way a museum would arrange its works of art. The smells and colors create the sensation of being immersed in a jungle. On the first pass of the shop, the plants appear the same, but no two things are alike. Everything is unique and eye-catching, especially the large twelve-foot monstera that visitors pass under to enter.

Vaughan herself is a bright, colorful, smiley, intelligent, passionate woman of color. She conducted this interview on her couch during February 2021 with nothing but laughs, smiles, red pajamas and a sense of hopefulness.

BEFORE THE PANDEMIC, Plant Salon was my "by-appointment-only" space, like a studio space. We had couches and things, so it was definitely comfortable. And even now with all of the plants and beauty products in a retail space, people just like to look. It's not like an in-and-out errand-running kind of spot. It's a spot. You do one pass and then another. Then you debate, *Do I need some candles? Do I even need this?*

I always liked thinking about that when I would go shopping to places like Anthropologie or just going downtown and in and out of stores: *How do I tend to shop?*

Back in the day, I spent the most time at places where I always got the most creative bang for my buck. A store like the old Barneys. We'd go in with braces and a backpack. Yeah, I was that person in high school. It was like visiting the museum, the same way you go to the Field Museum[104] and might stop and take in the little different exhibits.

VIRUS CITY

---

[104] Chicago's natural-history museum. https://www.fieldmuseum.org/

It was a department store where you would buy the $10,000 suit that had burned holes in it. Going to a shop like that and seeing these amazingly high-end batch designers, but then being able to go into the soap bar or plant section, to be able to get all the needs met in one place, that was fierce, you know? And then you might go home and be like, *My plants look lonely. I need to get some sticks or something to make more of a motif.*

It's not very often that you can find shops that don't just treat bath and beauty stuff as this little add-on. Barneys was more focused. So, I always thought, *Why isn't that a thing I can do? How do you tie beauty and plants together?* And that's how I think you start to make that little world at home. Because you were inspired by your favorite places.

:::::::::::::::

There's this thing called biophilia. It is a really neat way of having that marriage between how people interact in their space and the effect of nature on that person and their own sense of growth. It's bringing nature and nature's effect on the human experience. It's having nature in your living space.

There's a wonderful TED Talk from Bryan Stevenson, who helped design The National Memorial for Peace and Justice, the museum down South displaying the history of lynching.[105] Every aspect of the space is designed to impress upon you the weight of lynching, the culture, pain, and history. It's heavy. Even the way they designed the landscape so that as you approach the museum, it is surrounded by these posts coming out of the ground that symbolize trees and cast shadows in certain ways, shadows used to symbolize the number of bodies.

People try to bring biophilia into interior design and into interior decor, so you truly feel like you are inside of nature. Hilton Carter[106] is a great example of that. He tries to bring more into decor as a plant influencer. Like, how is this plant going to grow and interact with space there? He would say that if you enjoy this plant being on its side, put it on its side and enjoy the path of watching it grow.

I am very familiar with touching and manipulating materials in a space. I have a BFA from the School of the Art Institute [of Chicago] in materials studies. You take classes through sculptures, through ceramics, patch theory, a lot of fashion theory classes about how the body interacts with space.

Going into makeup and bridal arts, to me, was a nice extension. I have had three years with my other company, Nika Vaughan Bridal Artists. Instead of working bigger with sculpture, you're working smaller and finer. This very thin substance over another substance that has to interact between the two of them.

---

[105] The National Memorial for Peace and Justice opened in 2018 in Montgomery, Alabama. https://museum andmemorial.eji.org/memorial
[106] Hilton Carter is an influencer and interior designer known for featuring plants in his décor on Instagram.

In the wedding world, you're helping someone curate an event that has a high emotional value. So they should have a lot of say in what this looks like and it needs to project some part of them. And so, they hire the venue, and they hire hair and makeup, and they hire floral and event designers. It's almost like they're fabricating an environment.

Before the COVID-19 pandemic, Nika Vaughan Bridal Artists was doing national events. We were doing about two hundred weddings a year. Ninety-nine percent of my clients were white. And they were having $100,000 weddings.

I think when you're a Black person in that world you start to have this weird servitude, a déjà vu. Like, I need to set some clear boundaries because something about this dichotomy is a little messed up. The way that you speak to me is not as equals. And it's one thing when you are at someone's wedding and it's the best of the best. You cry with them and you've seen three thousand billion weddings, but still, this is beautiful.

Other weddings, you *are* the help. You are *literally* the help. And you're like, this is not my job description.

: : : : : : : :
: : : : : : : : : : : : • • •
: : : : : : : : : :

People asked me if I was ever going to sell plants in my bridal business. But, I thought, *No, that's weird. Not my thing.* I had only done these small plant pop-ups because plants make babies, and you need to get rid of some or you run out of space.

And then the pandemic came. The writing on the wall was that weddings were not coming back anytime soon. Then I didn't know how I was going to pay the rent with just the wedding business.

So in April of 2020, I opened Plant Salon in the West Town area. I was so basic naming it. I was just like...Plant Salon! It actually was a little bit of a plant district already. And that was very freeing for me because I felt safe exploring the whole self-care-beauty-Black-plants thing. Plant Salon is much freer. I have more of my own voice in it. I am the owner.

Plus, I can't take these plants home. I own a Prius!

I have a large monstera plant in the window at Plant Salon. People would roll in and go, "Oh, I want this, I want this, I want this. Yeah. I'll take one of those." And they're pointing to my monstera. So, I was like, "That's ten grand," the exaggerated 2020 pandemic price. That's being generous. And they pause. And you should pause!

I got that tree from an estate sale, maybe three years ago at this point. I don't even think it was that old. The diameter of the original pot was like fourteen inches, if that. [The owner] had a bunch of rocks in it to help pull it up, but it was only like three or four feet tall, and it was rolling sideways because she lived in this dark little bungalow and the poor thing was just looking for light. I literally could lift it with one hand and put it in my Prius. I potted it vertically in my space. And it was probably about as tall as me when it was in the pot. That's about five feet maybe.

And, oh, it grew. We had to repot it twice. Now it is in a thirty-inch pot, and it reaches our ceiling at about twelve-plus feet. The one that I got just happened to be very large from the process of air layering, which means propagating a new plant from an established plant. And instead of just taking a cutting and sticking it in water or dirt and going, "Please, I hope roots grow," layering is a great way to ensure it survives.

It is a very expensive plant to me. So yes, it's definitely a [seller's] market for that baby. She's mine. Even if I had to move. I don't know where or how I would move it, but she is gonna be with me for a minute.

······
·········
········

When you're an entrepreneur who lives and breathes entrepreneurship, in maybe a not-so-healthful way, you plan innovations for when you take over the world. You're still dumping the garbage yourself. You're still all hands in. And that to me has been huge.

The Black Lives Matter protest, with the focus on violence against Black people and the marches, had a huge impact on Plant Salon. Our biggest fear was when they were breaking windows in the riots. And luckily, I think a lot of the people that were engaging in that in our community were trying to, at least in their rage, be discerning of small businesses, you know? I had people who knew that I sold plants. 'Cause I'm like, it's a plant shop. I cannot do this.

Then all of a sudden, the attention turns to how do you support Black Lives Matter. With signs? Maybe you don't really have a connection? They were literally using Black Lives Matter signs as "Don't break my window" signs. And so, I didn't put anything up in my window because I was like, "I'm the one sweeping the floor here. You should know that. I'm on your side. Me, I'm your sign."

Being located where we were was a path for a lot of protests and marches that went up and down the community. On Ashland, they had thirty thousand people.[107] And we had people come back saying, "I saw this when I was marching, and I said, I'm going to come back here." All of that really helped fuel the momentum of people paying attention to our shop.

---

[107] https://abc7chicago.com/chicago-protest-black-lives-matter-peaceful-police-brutality/6225272/

I'd say it's a blessing and a curse, because then you have people who want to do something. They want to shop at this Black-owned business. I would have people come in and pick up plants and then go, "Are you the owner?" "Yes, I am Black, and I am the owner." And for them that was the whole point of shopping there: I am open, and I am Black.

I had friends that were very bothered I was open to the public, saying it's not safe. I was like, "Look, if this is not the activity for you, then there's curbside pickup." But if their one excursion outside of their bubble is going to be Trader Joe's and the nearby plant shop, and then they're back in their house for two, three days, I felt safe with that. That felt OK for me. But that was definitely a conversation.

• • • • • • • •
• • • • • • • • • • • •
• • • • • • • • •

When I opened Plant Salon, I worked there 24/7 and even overnight. I was there by myself. I would sleep there, and it was just all-consuming to the point where your family gets concerned. I'm eating a lot of fast food in my car, and I'm kind of always a little bit in pain. I'd be at Plant Salon watering plants and stuff, thinking I had to hire some employees, because remote learning was coming back. I do have two 8-year-olds.

Before the pandemic, I could work early and had all the time to go meet the school bus. *Oh, how inconvenient. I have to be home by three in the afternoon now.* But now it's comical. I mean, with the pandemic, we had like a tent of blankets and chairs in the back of my shop and the smell of McDonald's wafting.

One of the battles of dealing with COVID and being a parent is you have to partic-ipate in your world. I have friends from the wedding business who had been out of work. Like, they've just been out of work this whole time. I couldn't imagine. There's a whole other life besides just the project you're working on. It's already hard when you're an artist and you want to do what you do 24/7. But then your partner or your family go, "Hi, remember us?" Your pets are like, "Hi, it me!" That's how bad this is.

I'm recognizing I need help. Checking in with a therapist, just even when it's like, "We got nothing to talk about today. Tell me what happened this week. 'Cause I know something did, and it's so much to process." And I will try to do things like sit in my own shop and have that experience with it when no one else is there.

I sent [my kids] back to school because I thought that was what was best for them. There are only two kids who've chosen to go back at this time in each classroom. So, they're one of two kids in their own classroom.

I think it's a benefit for them. I wanted them to ease back into it a little bit. That's been our big lesson: not pretending that even though we all are talking about this new normal, that this is the new normal. It's still awkward, uncomfortable and unsettling, and *stressful*.

I talk about it with them. "You're probably going to remember this time period for the rest of your life, and it's weird." When they had their first day back officially, it was super inconvenient. Like, how do you work? How do you come and go with that? But we'll check in and ask, "How do you feel today? 'Cause it was weird. You don't have to pretend it wasn't."

We talk about that as a family. We have a crisis. There's the getting through the crisis and then there's once the crisis is over. That's when you process the crisis. Right? So, at some point this is going to feel over. And then the real angst of it is going to hit home. And the stress of it is going to hit.

The most impacted were people that have not left their house still. That was odd because it's like part of your network and part of you, the people that I checked in with who are like, "Nope, I'm done. I'm in my house." "Nope. I don't see people and I barely Zoom."

And when you would see them, you can just tell looking at them that like, *No, you never got sick, but I feel like COVID got you some way.*

—TONI McELRATH

Sitting Ducks

JAMES SWANSEY, PROGRAM APPRENTICE

James Swansey, a Future Leaders Apprenticeship Program apprentice at Restore Justice Illinois, was only 18 when he was sentenced to natural life with no parole for murder. Through resentencing, Swansey's time was shortened to twenty-eight years, which he spent both at Menard Correctional Center in Chester and at Stateville Correctional Center, a maximum-security facility in Crest Hill, Illinois.

Listed as one of the most crowded jails in Illinois with more than one thousand men incarcerated,[108] Stateville was one of the prisons in the state most heavily impacted by COVID-19, with more than 13 percent of its population infected by June 24, 2020.[109] Tests were not readily available, and PPE was scarce. Swansey recalls how the new normal set in as inmates became infected and were placed in quarantine or taken to the hospital, some never returning.

More than four months after his release, Swansey reflected on his time at Stateville, being released into a world of isolation and social distancing, and the small moments that have brought him joy.

WHEN THE PANDEMIC FIRST HIT in March [2020], I was in the first cellhouse that got put on quarantine. They didn't know what was going on. Guys were getting fevers—one guy had a fever of, like, 107 degrees—and so they put him in a cellhouse. But they didn't know what it was.

It was crazy. They put us down for ten days under quarantine and nothing came of it because they weren't testing. They didn't start testing 'til months down the line, so nobody really knew what it was, and nobody really could tell us why we were in quarantine. All we knew was that we couldn't go anywhere because we were on medical quarantine.

At first, people didn't take it seriously, because anything that has us locked in a cell, we're gonna fight. Guys want to get out.

---

[108] Source: https://www2.illinois.gov/idoc/facilities/Pages/statevillecorrectionalcenter.aspx
[109] Source: https://www.chicagoreporter.com/forgotten-stateville-inmates-warn-of-rising-covid-19-outbreak-behind-bars/

After ten days, they took us off and put the cellhouse next door under quarantine, which basically consisted of the elder people with ailments and illnesses and underlying conditions. Things took a turn for the worse, and that's when guys realized it was serious. It was instant. Once they put that cellhouse on quarantine, people started going to the outside hospital left and right.

Guys got sick, and then we learned that they had started passing. Five or six dead guys that a lot of us knew. That really hit home 'cause this same individual that you just saw two weeks ago had just perished due to this pandemic.

It got serious really quick. Guys didn't know how to handle it. It was a mixture of being angry that you got stuck in the cell and, of course, you can't socially distance in the penitentiary. I wouldn't say it was tough, but it was scary. You really didn't know what to expect. You just wanted to keep yourself as safe as possible.

During quarantine, medical staff started coming by and checking everybody's temperature. Anybody that had a high temperature, they would move them. They didn't tell you why; they didn't tell you where you were going. They didn't say anything like that.

Guys really started to make noise and wanted to talk to the administration, because we were sitting ducks. We're in a cellhouse with no air circulating, and there's this virus that can kill you. More or less, we were stuck.

PPE stuff came in after the governor got on TV. At that point, so many people from Stateville were being transported to the outside hospital that it sent guys back to the penitentiary. That's when the government got involved and the National Guard came down.[110]

For guys in the cell, they just gave you a mask once a week, gave you soap, and passed down hand sanitizer. The staff would walk around with a bottle of it while the nurse handed the meds out. They would also come around before they served the food and give guys a chance to use the sanitizer.

It got better over time. Those who had jobs and things of that nature had access to PPE because they went out and about. I had a job, so I definitely had it.

I worked in the tunnel group. Stateville is made up of a series of tunnels that get you wherever you need to go. My responsibility was to keep these tunnels clean, so I had access all over the joint. I could move around, and I also was able to keep myself safe because I had access to the gloves, the PPE gear, the mask, the shields, everything.

---

[110] Illinois governor J.B. Pritzer sent thirty National Guard members to help with the Stateville outbreak on April 2, 2020. Source: https://wgntv.com/news/coronavirus/gov-pritzker-sends-national-guard-to-stateville-to-help-with-covid-19-outbreak/

If you showed any symptoms, or if you complained of any symptoms, they quarantined you. They made you take all your property and sent you to a separate cell. After fourteen days, the doctor would come and ask if you had those same symptoms still. If you said you were all right, they cleared you and put you right back in the same cell.

I knew a few people who caught the virus. Some of them tested positive but felt like they didn't have any symptoms. Still, they ended up quarantined and labeled as asymptomatic. I was blessed enough to never be in that situation, at least that I know of.

It was difficult, especially at first. Testing didn't start until maybe August [2020], so we went a long time without it. The more coverage Stateville got, the more people started realizing the situation, and they made it so that workers had to get tested. It went from getting tested once every month to every two weeks. I'm still in touch with a lot of guys there, and they say that they test everybody now. It's not just specific people; they test everybody every three days. It's gotten better.

· · · · · · ·
· · · · · · · · · · ·
· · · · · · · · · ·

I came home December 9, 2020. I did twenty-eight years. It was maybe about a month short of twenty-eight years, but inside we always round up. It's a big difference, being locked in the cell as opposed to being in an apartment or house. Believe it or not, [lockdown at home] was a step up.

I understand it's a pandemic, but coming from where I came from, I'm enjoying every minute of it while staying safe and understanding and respecting people's space, because everybody has a different point of view.

I'm a big people person, so I like being around others. Last week, we went to the Chicago Premium Outlet Mall in Aurora, and that alone was just awesome. There were so many people. Some that had a mask on, and some that didn't, but it's more or less what you want to do as an individual. I just want to go out and enjoy life.

The fact that I can leave the house right now—just put my mask on, hop in the car, and drive somewhere—that's more than I really thought that I would be doing. I'm enjoying it, and I know it's only gonna get better.

I think the biggest change is talking to and seeing people that sometimes struggled to visit me or waited on my call. But the biggest thing for me is talking to my mother every day. Just the fact that she can cook for me—she'll cook for me five times a day! It's just automatic, and that's one thing that I never try to take from her. When she says, "Are you hungry?" I always say yes.

I have two siblings, a younger brother and a younger sister, but she calls me the baby because I was gone for so long. The simple fact that I can enjoy family now is the best thing. I just love having a good time. I love to laugh, and that's what I'm able to do.

I can sit around all day with my family and just talk or watch TV. My mother is a movie buff, so she loves to watch movies. I have no problem with that. I just love being able to stay in touch with people without having to wait for a response to a letter.

∷∷∷∷∷•••
∷∷∷∷∷

Right now, I'm an apprentice in the Future Leaders Apprentice Program run by Mr. Wendell Robinson, the program manager at Restore Justice. We were incarcerated together, and when he got out four years ago, he ended up working there. He was the first apprentice.

I always told him that was something I would love to do because I love to talk. I love to inspire. I love to give people hope. It gives guys the chance to really see that there are good things that can come out of imprisonment. Hearing it from me, it validates it because they know I did a lot of time, so there's no reason for me to bullshit them. I'm gonna give it to them straight.

The whole premise of Restore Justice is to end long-term incarceration. We're trying to bring parole back; we're trying to end the juvenile life period. We're trying to make it so if you're 21 years or younger, you can see the parole board. We're just trying to make sure they can't lock you up and throw away the key.

Everybody makes mistakes. People deserve help, a chance to make a difference. A lot of guys on the inside don't know that they have so many people fighting for them, and I think that's the one thing that intrigued me the most about Restore Justice. There are a lot of people that want to give people second chances.

My favorite part is being able to have a voice. I can tell my story firsthand, I guess you could say, because this is something that I experienced, and this is something that I can pass on to people that can make a difference. I've also become that individual that can make a difference. I can help those still behind the wall. That's what I enjoy most—being able to change things.

You never know who you're gonna make a difference for. You never know who might see your story. It's just me being me, and that's the biggest advice that Wendell gave me before I started the apprenticeship. Just be yourself; show people who you are, who you've become. Show them that you're not the individual that committed that horrific crime—and I'm not.

You have to be able to put other people before you. Being in the penitentiary definitely taught me patience and understanding for that. You must be mentally strong. It's always easy to do the bad thing. It's hard to do the right thing, but it's more satisfying. I was a little young dude, and I made some bad decisions that ultimately took me away from everybody that loved me. I did twenty-eight years, and everybody that loved me did twenty-eight years too.

You learn not to follow the crowd. You learn not to do what the next individual did just because you think it's cool. You learn to not be susceptible to peer pressure. Although I made the worst mistake of my life, being away taught me so much about me and other people and the world itself. I'm proud of the individual that I've become, so I'll pay it forward. I want to show guys that it's possible—it's possible to come home and do the right thing.

It is possible to hit the ground running and make a difference.

—MARIA MAYNEZ

A former college debate champion, Conley was a good speaker with a penchant for seeing the pandemic through a historical perspective.

The Lens of History

JIM CONLEY, TEACHER

Jim Conley, a world history teacher at Morton Freshman Center in Cicero, Illinois, was sitting in his kitchen, though his students were never far from his mind. Cicero, a heavily Latinx suburb just west of Chicago, was the site of two shooting deaths[111] that occurred in the wake of the death of George Floyd and the unrest that followed.

It was midday on February 20, 2021, and Conley kept shifting his laptop to adjust the lighting on his end of the Zoom call from his home in Chicago's Logan Square neighborhood. Over his shoulder, I could see his wife rummaging in the fridge. A former college debate champion, Conley was a good speaker with a penchant for seeing the pandemic through a historical perspective.

I TEACH WORLD HISTORY to freshmen.

The classical way that you teach world history is very Eurocentric. A typical world history class starts at Greece, proceeds to Rome, gets to the Middle Ages, goes to the Renaissance, then into the modern world after that. Everything is through the lens of a European focus. If you do talk about other cultures at all, it is through the lens of how Europeans interact with them.

I have done everything that I can to push my department into thinking about teaching world history far more thematically, far more through the lens of "let's take a theme that appears in a particular time period of history and then see how that plays out in a number of different regions around the planet." Otherwise, the perspective that kids can get is distorted.

I have to relate it to their lives somehow. If it's just some dry factoid from history, they'll tune out. Ultimately, the bottom line is that I want to get them to talk and to write. It doesn't really matter so much that they learn about Napoleon's campaigns in Russia. I could care less. And they probably could too. It's really about getting them to speak better and write better. That's my end goal. Everything else is a tool, an entry point to get them into that mindset.

---

[111] On June 1, 2020, more than sixty people were arrested during the unrest in Cicero. Four people were shot. Two Chicago residents, Jose Gutierrez, 28, and Victor Cazares Jr., 27, died from their injuries. Source: https://www.fox32chicago.com/news/2-killed-over-60-arrested-in-cicero-as-protests-turn-violent

The teaching piece has been challenging during this entire span.

My school is called the Morton Freshman Center in Cicero. We teach exclusively freshmen—ninth graders, 14, 15 years old. Our population is 98 percent Latino. It's been a while since I've looked at the free and reduced-price lunch percentage, but I think we're at, like, 80 percent. It might be higher now. It's an economically challenged community in a lot of ways. And the population of students that I have reflects that.

Initially, a lot of teachers thought [remote learning] was going to be short. I remember, before our spring break [in March 2020], we all thought we'd be back right afterward. We have a very far-sighted superintendent who decided that we needed to have our kids exposed to technology far more than you would expect out of an urban district. Each kid, when they come in, gets a laptop. And so we were good to go, from a technology standpoint. In that way, it's been OK.

A lot of our students, given the demographics and the financial challenges, have internet connectivity issues, though. That's been a challenge for some of our kids.

There was, in the summer, a gigantic debate about whether or not teachers should come back into the building. My union[112] decided not to fight it very hard. They made the decision that we teachers would go into the building and teach from school. There was a lot of consternation about that. A lot of teachers disagreed with it. I was happy to get back into school and be teaching from the classroom.

We started hybrid on February 1, 2021, and the first week I had a few kids come in. It was typically about one kid per class. Then the weather hit, and attendance just fell off a cliff. With the weather getting better, kids are starting to come back in. But again, no more than, like, one kid in a class.

I also don't know from day to day if that kid is actually going to come into the school. I'll see that kid who signed up for hybrid one time a week and then the rest of the week I won't see him. So, yeah, I won't lie, hybrid is really hard, especially to structure something for the vast majority of your kids who are remote and then the one kid who's there.

A lot of kids don't want to turn their cameras on, especially at the age of 14. Some of it's just an age-related issue. They're at an age where they're shy and embarrassed. And in a lot of cases, they're living in conditions that are challenging to show live on camera.

112 Cicero Council is the teachers' union serving Morton and other Cicero-area schools.

A lot of my kids are taking care of brothers and sisters at the same time that they're trying to log in for my class. So as much as possible, I try to design lessons that I can present live but that they can log on later and see at their convenience.

It's oftentimes very difficult to know if a kid is actually there or if they've just logged on and they're "there," but perhaps they're off doing something else.

I always start out every class with a social-emotional component. I'll ask how their day is. There's about ten minutes of time at the start of class that I'll block off for them to express what they're feeling and what their emotions are. With the switch to remote, I find myself having to do a lot more lectures, a lot more direct teaching, and then, when possible, having kids do breakout rooms and discussions as much as I can. They'll use the [Zoom] chat a lot. It has kind of become teaching by chat.

In normal school, you'd typically have a very chaotic, rowdy classroom. Now it's very quiet. But they will chat. They will type out their feelings, their emotions, what's going on in their lives. The girls are starting to turn 15, so they're talking about their *quinceañeras*. And the boys are getting ready to start driver's ed. They're on and on about their favorite rap group or their favorite performer. They're all still interested in those kinds of things.

So, while they're not willing to go on camera, they are willing to share a lot more personal things in the chat than they ever would have done in person. That's the biggest difference, I would say. Privately, they've shared struggles as far as death and sickness and other things that have come along with COVID. And that's how I've learned about some of their individual challenges.

I had a boy who was infuriated by his mother not wanting to quarantine. She tested positive and wouldn't quarantine. She just went on about her life, you know. But at the same time, she's got to work. If you have a factory job that won't let you take off, you can't afford to take off.

A lot of my parents are very afraid of sending kids back, given the current COVID numbers. But even as the COVID numbers have been decreasing, there's still a lot of hesitancy to send kids back fully. We haven't had to deal with a lot of the vicious political fights that have taken place between the parents who are like, "No, we have to be fully remote" or "No, we have to fully open up." It's not really been that challenging for my district compared to the New Triers[113] of the world and some of the other districts. It's very easy, I think, for people from [privileged]

[113] New Trier Township High School in Winnetka, Illinois, serves some of the wealthiest communities in the Chicago area. It reports only 4 percent economically disadvantaged students, as opposed to 91 percent economically disadvantaged at Morton in Cicero. Sources: https://www.usnews.com/education/best-high-schools/illinois/districts/new-trier-township-high-school-district-203/new-trier-township-high-school-winnetka-153386 / and https://www.usnews.com/education/best-high-schools/illinois/districts/j-s-morton-high-school-district-201/j-sterling-morton-east-high-sch-153385

demographics to say, "What's the problem? Why wouldn't you want to send your kid back in?" But to be honest, those communities haven't been hit as hard as parents from Cicero have been.

At one point we were up to, I think, a 14 percent positivity rate. We had a huge outbreak in an assisted living facility in Cicero.[114] Just by the nature of the housing situation in Cicero—which is oftentimes very crowded, and where it is difficult for parents to socially distance—the spread has been fairly extensive. A lot of my parents and a lot of the community work in the increasing warehouse economy of the area.

There's a gigantic bakery that opened up in Cicero. There's an Amazon warehouse there. A lot of my parents can't work from home.

And I've had kids who've lost their parents. Pretty much every week, they'll have some sort of death in the family.

There's a program that we use to track absences. The excuse of COVID I've seen at least once every single week since we started. And a lot of kids are saying, you know, "It was my grandmother, my aunt, my mom. I'm going to need some time."

•••••• ••••
••••••••••••
•••••••••

This year has been a huge challenge, both with COVID and with the Black Lives Matter movement. [Chicago Mayor] Lori Lightfoot lives not too far from me,[115] so I got to see firsthand a lot of the protests happening. Right in front of Lori Lightfoot's house, there was just a phalanx of police officers that closed down our entire section of the neighborhood to protesters.

It was basically the entire summer that the neighborhood kind of felt like a fortress. There was a lot of police presence, and there were several different protests that were going on at that time. It seems like everything hit at one moment, from COVID to Black Lives Matter to some of the other issues that were going on. There was a solid month and a half in June [2020], heading into July, that was just exhausting, for lack of a better word.

Cicero Avenue is sort of the dividing line between the Lawndale neighborhood [of Chicago] and Cicero. And there's a fairly stark racial/ethnic dividing line at that street. Lawndale is majority African American.[116] Cicero is absolutely major-ity Latino.[117] However, especially with the housing crisis that's happened since

114 Source: https://www.nbcchicago.com/news/coronavirus/cicero-nursing-home-faces-lawsuit-as-more-than-200-residents-diagnosed-with-coronavirus/2266575/

115 Lightfoot, like Conley, lives in the Logan Square neighborhood on Chicago's Northwest Side.
Source: https://blockclubchicago.org/2019/03/29/lori-lightfoot-on-why-she-chose-to-live-in-logan-square-and-how-living-there-shaped-her-worldview/

116 Source: https://interactive.wttw.com/chicago-by-l/neighborhoods/north-lawndale

117 Source: https://www.census.gov/quickfacts/cicerotownillinois

I've been teaching, the amount of affordable housing in Chicago has started to decrease. And a lot of that has been either market-driven or the social inequity—getting rid of traditional public housing, you know, bringing down Cabrini,[118] for instance, or Henry Horner.[119] And then that whole policy of giving rent vouchers to people and saying, "Just go wherever you can to find a house."

There has been an increasing amount of African American families moving into Cicero over that time. It's slow and gradual, but it's definitely been apparent. Like I said, 98 percent of our kids are Latino, but those two percent I was just talking about are African American. There is legit racial tension in Cicero and in that sort of dividing line of Cicero Avenue between the two.

A lot of teachers think if, in a US history class, I talk about slavery, I've done my "Black" lesson for that particular unit, and I can move on. But stripped of its context—if that's [the only lesson]—kids can get a terrible perspective about Black contributions to America. And then the story will pick up again with the civil rights movement and Martin Luther King.

That's the perspective that a lot of Americans get. That can sometimes be an even more dangerous perspective than just leaving African American history out altogether, because, again, taking that approach can get people to think of this long march to progress.

So fast-forward to the Black Lives Matter movement and the protests that happened over the summer [of 2020]. I didn't have classes going on at that moment. However, I still kept in contact with a lot of my old students who were becoming sophomores over the summer. They were absolutely communicating to me their anxieties over those several nights that things really exploded.

It was really hard. There was a lot of looting, especially on that border line on Cicero Avenue. Cermak and Cicero is the site of a lot of different strip malls and family-owned businesses—a lot of restaurants, places that serve the *quinceañera* market, etc. They got hit really hard, and that caused a lot of racial tension. There's a liquor store right on that corner. There were people with guns on the roof, trying to make sure that nobody broke in. A few people died in the violence in Cicero. It was really hard.

The night after the worst of it, our superintendent organized a community cleanup for that next morning. A lot of teachers came out to help the community clean up. The next day after that cleanup, the city of Cicero organized a peace march through the town and that calmed things down quite a bit.[120]

118 The Cabrini-Green housing projects on Chicago's North Side. Source: https://www.britannica.com/topic/Cabrini-Green
119 The Henry Horner Homes on Chicago's Near West Side were dismantled between the late 1990s and early 2000s. Source: https://www.chicagoreporter.com/dismantling-the-towers/
120 A group of Cicero residents organized a unity march on June 7, 2020, as a response to the June 1 incidents.

But, yeah, there were moments that were really scary. The kids really don't talk about it that much.

● ● ● ● ● ● ●
● ● ● ● ● ● ● ● ● ● ●
● ● ● ● ● ● ● ● ●

I think most people have navigated all this craziness as best they can. I look at things through the lens of history, and given my reading of history and the past, I think people have generally done the best they can in adapting to change.

The closest comparison [to now] would be the immediate post–World War I years. The Spanish flu[121] obviously gets a lot of attention, so there's that pandemic connection. But at the same time, there were a lot of racial tensions that were going on in that moment that are very comparable to what's going on now.

We're kind of repeating the interwar years in a lot of ways, not just here in America, but globally as well. Some of the same exact kind of tensions between the global perspective you saw in the League of Nations[122] at that time to a much more hypernationalistic perspective that you saw in, say, Italy and Germany and the America First movement[123] during that time—you're seeing some of the same things repeat again.

I think [knowing history] can definitely help a person navigate things if you see how other humans have done it.

● ● ● ● ● ● ●
● ● ● ● ● ● ● ● ● ● ●
● ● ● ● ● ● ● ● ●

It's going to be a lot of work coming back from all this, getting kids back into the mentality of school. It's going to be a big challenge, even apart from getting people comfortable being around each other again—you know, even leaving vaccinations off the table, just getting kids back into a routine of doing school and having that as a separate reality from home.

In some ways, kids are having the same challenges that adults are; their worlds are coming together like never before. For parents, it's the work world and the home world coming together. For kids, it's the school world and the home world coming together too. Separating those two worlds is going to be the biggest challenge moving forward.

—PAIGE GILBERG

---

121 The 1918 Spanish flu pandemic killed an estimated fifty million people worldwide, 675,000 of them in the United States. Source: https://www.cdc.gov/flu/pandemic-resources/1918-pandemic-h1n1.html
122 The League of Nations was established in the wake of World War I to maintain world peace.
Source: https://www.un.org/en/about-us/history-of-the-un/predecessor
123 The American First Committee was established to pressure the United States to stay out of World War II.
Source: https://www.cfr.org/blog/history-lessons-america-first-committee-forms

If I Bumped into My Freshmen on the Street

"GENEVIEVE," TEACHER

In February 2021, nearly one year after the COVID-19 lockdowns in the United States, Chicago Public Schools (CPS) announced dates for K–8 students to return to school. Tensions were high as members of the Chicago Teachers Union (CTU) fought against returning to in-person classes over safety concerns. Although elementary and middle schools were in the process of reopening, no date had been set for high school students to return to in-person school. Instead of striking, CTU members voted for a remote work action—to continue doing work, but remotely.[124]

Genevieve (not her real name) is a history teacher at a small, unnamed public high school on Chicago's West Side. In 2021, she was in her third year teaching at this school, but her seventh year in the district. After finishing up some end-of-the-week work, she logged onto Zoom to give an interview about her experience as an educator during the COVID-19 pandemic.

Genevieve was wearing a red Chicago Teachers Union zip-up. The white CTU crest spoke volumes about where her loyalties lay in the fight for reopening schools. Genevieve told it the way it was. There was no real malice in her words, just hurt and frustration.

I DIDN'T BECOME A TEACHER to sit at a computer. I didn't become a teacher to talk to myself. That is really what my day is now, sitting on a computer talking to myself. Maybe occasionally somebody responds. [I'm] really missing the human element.

I'm at a very small school, so I teach freshmen and sophomores. At least I know what my sophomores mostly look like because I had them last year in person. I have no idea who my freshmen are. If I bumped into my freshmen on the street, they would recognize me, but I would not know what they look like.

Apparently last year's senior class, when they had remote learning in the spring, was super chatty in the chat box. And I was just like, "That would be nice." All the senior teachers were like, "Oh, my God, they're so distracted."

---

[124]https://www.chicagotribune.com/news/breaking/ct-chicago-teachers-union-vote-remote-learning-teachers-20210124-ftdd3rzzorfnvglfnkgusm3q5m-story.html

Yeah, but at least they're being human. I don't know if I'm teaching humans!

High school students, by and large, don't turn their cameras on. Maybe at some schools they do, but my school is not one of those. I have maybe four students that will once in a blue moon turn their microphone on and say something. I've seen one student this year on camera.

The struggle of teaching is to get your students to pay attention. When you're at home, there's just so many distractions, and you don't know when a student is paying attention and when they are not. In the classroom, it's fairly obvious. Here, I will call a student's name a few times and they may not respond, and it's like, *OK, so is the volume low? Is the room really loud? Did they go to the bathroom? Did they fall asleep?* I have zero, *zero* idea of what happens on their end.

Kids are kids, and they're not going to do what they're supposed to do all the time. Most parents are working parents, so they can't really keep an eye on them all the time. Someone can wake up their student for their first class, but if they don't attend the other six, what are [we] going to do about it?

In a lot of the cases, the students who need a lot of support are frequently MIA. [Some] students attend my class once a week and don't do any work, and we don't have an email address for their parents, and their parents don't pick up the phone. Or we have a student whose family doesn't have a phone anymore. With[out] being in the building, the students who have shifty attendance in person are really falling through [the cracks].

. . . .
. . . .
. . . .

The school is in Little Village. Almost all my students are from Mexican immigrant families. I would say about 35 percent of the school are English-language learners. Their conversational English is fine, but their academic language is not good enough to test out [of] the program.[125]

We only have fifteen teachers, which is quite a lot for who and what we are. In an ideal world, we are a three-year high school. Students take classes year-round. They have summer school. If they don't fail any courses in high school, they will graduate in three years.

That said, a lot of our students do end up taking four years because they need to retake classes or do credit recovery. Little Village is super low income,[126] and the school reflects that. We're kind of a forgotten school. We have our offices and

---

125 Source: https://www.cps.edu/academics/language-and-culture/english-learners-program/
126 Per-capita income in Little Village is $11,000—about a third as much as the average for the rest of the city—and about 35 percent of the neighborhood's residents live in poverty. Source: https://littlevillage communityportal.org/lv-community/today/

computer lab in the basement of an elementary school, and we rent space from the Boys and Girls Club down the block. It's a bad space for a school.

There are all these things I didn't realize when I started working at the school. School buildings are built in a specific way. The halls are fairly wide, enough to allow many people to pass, the bathrooms are bigger, and there are lockers and stuff. Classrooms *should* be a certain size.

That is not what we have in this building. So, in normal times, we do a lot of walking back and forth between buildings and making do with less-than-ideal facilities.

• • • • • • • •
• • • • • • • • • • •
• • • • • • • • •

I don't go into the classroom these days. I know there are teachers who have taught from school buildings because their internet is not great at home, but everyone I know at my school has been home.

The district hasn't yet announced a date for high schools to come back in person. I don't know what they're planning, although I feel like it's nefarious based on past experience. My colleagues and I don't know what's going to happen if they do announce a date because all the safety measures that are supposed to be done for COVID can't be done at our school with the way that the building is.

This isn't going to work.

They did all these ventilation assessments. I don't know much about ventilation and the COVID standards around it, but they went to all of the rooms that we use in both buildings and were like, "OK, does this room have a working HVAC[127] system and a window that opens?" If it has one of those two, it passes their safety test, which I think is horrible.

They listed about fifteen rooms that we have, which may include some of our offices, and only seven or eight of those passed the tests. Pretty low bar to begin with. Lots of them don't even have windows and don't have a working HVAC system. The only room that has both is a bathroom.

But they're saying—on this website[128] where they put all this data—[that schools are] safe to open, and rooms that aren't safe shouldn't be used.

But then when you go on the page for my school, the report is mysteriously just missing. Not there. So because it's not there, they can say that we're safe? We can't open a school with less than half of our classrooms usable.

---

[127] Heating, ventilation, and air-conditioning system
[128] https://www.cps.edu/services-and-supports/school-facilities/air-quality-testing/

The district and the higher-ups aren't really working on this at all. They're leaving it to the principals. My principal, if you like doing your own thing, he's great. When you need him to run stuff and delegate and make decisions, he's awful. He's paralyzed right now because we're in a pandemic and he doesn't know what to do normally. We have a few teachers who have stepped up to try and figure this out, but it's an impossible task.

They reached a deal between CPS and CTU.[129] I am *not* a fan of the deal.[130]

There were things that we were pushing for when we started resisting actively against the district [at] the beginning of January. A lot of those things were not in this proposal. I voted against it when it was put to a vote before the membership, but a lot of people felt that it was the best that we could get. That was the message that came from our union leadership. I'm still kind of grumpy at them for that.

Until the middle of January, the district was saying, "We don't have to negotiate return with you because there was this law put on the books in the '90s that said that CTU can only go on strike for pay and benefits."[131]

It wasn't a law that applied to any other union in the state, just us. They essentially stonewalled the union for most of [2020–2021]. And then, when we had the remote-work vote, all of a sudden, they were like, oh, maybe we should take you seriously, and they started putting forth a lot more offers and concessions than they had in the past.

But we also had a mayor who was doing a lot of gaslighting and straight-up lying, so I think that by the time we got to the end of January, our union leaders were just like, "We don't know if we can get a better deal."

Five weeks of wondering if we would go on strike was exhausting. I can't remember the last time I saw a *Chicago Tribune* article that portrayed teachers or especially the CTU in a positive light.

Occasionally there's an article about an individual teacher who's portrayed positively. It's a superhero discourse, like, "They put in so much time and so much effort and do these amazing things that no one else is doing," and therefore we

---

129 Source: https://www.ctulocal1.org/posts/ctu-rank-and-file-vote-to-approve-tentative-agreement/
130 CTU teachers and CPS leadership clashed over when to bring back students for in-person learning, how to accommodate teachers with increased health risks, and COVID-19 mitigation strategies in their buildings, among others. After the ratification of the tentative agreement on February 10, 2021, CTU members submitted a no-confidence vote against CPS and Chicago Mayor Lori Lightfoot. Source: https://www.chicagotribune.com/coronavirus/ct-ctu-delegates-tentative-reopening-deal-20210209-ch74mqecqfdpzpqmnof4qij6ke-story.html
131 The Illinois Educational Labor Relations Act was passed to regulate Illinois Teacher's Unions' strikes. Source: https://www.illinoispolicy.org/faqs-what-chicago-teachers-should-know-before-going-on-strike/

should applaud them. But if you don't put in all that time and effort, then you're just seen as kind of less than. It would be nice if the world would stop demonizing us.

It's a national discourse around demonizing teachers. It's rooted in misogyny. It's rooted in capitalism. It's rooted in those discourses that if you love your job, then you should not demand adequate pay for what you do, that if you are part of the caring professions, then you do it because you love it, and therefore you shouldn't argue for things like better working conditions or benefits or better pay.

•••••••••••
•••••••••••••
•••••••••••

The more I hear about them saying [students will return for in-person learning], the more I'm like, you guys are just going to throw safety out the window and make us do it regardless of whether it's a safe or good idea. I feel like months ago this would have alarmed me.

Now this is what's going to happen. And it shouldn't happen, but we've given up. [We've] lost all of the influence that we really have over the process.

We're already seeing lots of shady stuff, [teachers] who received health accommodations for themselves or their family members being told, "We're offering you the vaccine, but just so you know, once you have the second vaccine, you'll be expected to come into the building." And you're like, but you gave me an accommodation to work from home!

That doesn't even take into account the fact that only 30 percent of students, if that, are coming into the building. They're doing all this pushing and all this effort for a small percentage of students who are mostly white and wealthy and will be OK if they stay home for the rest of the year.

•••••••••
•••••••••••
•••••••••

This may sound horrible, but I'm a lot less concerned with the long-term academic and educational implications than I am with the social, emotional, mental implications. You can't learn if you're traumatized. That's what it comes down to. And this year has been super traumatic for everybody.

There's this focus on what you can do for your own self-care, but emphasizing self-care is only putting a Band-Aid on a wound that's bleeding heavily. It doesn't change the systems that are creating the problem. It's just expecting you to deal with it on your own and somehow survive without becoming the burnt-out teacher. I think we've all reached that point this year, and self-care isn't solving that.

I do imagine returning to the building, coming back to normal. But when I stop and think about it, I know there are going to be so many things that no one can predict that students will be dealing with.

VIRUS CITY

That was probably in February [2020] when I started getting anxious. I started looking at the materials that were coming from China to understand how maybe we could prepare locally, but you're trying not to be an alarmist.

In March, we went into lockdown. Then I started questioning how we were individually preparing. I think I was one of the first people in my hospital to say, "This thing is probably airborne, and we should probably all be wearing N95s all the time."

Until that point, I was still seeing it as something that people who traveled would bring [back]. My very first patient—I think he was the index case at UIC—was a gentleman who had traveled to Europe for business and came in with symptoms that we later confirmed were COVID.

At the time, we couldn't get tested that quickly, so I didn't know until a week later, but I wondered how many other people he had interacted with in the process of traveling.

Around that same time, I got a call from a friend whose husband worked at O'Hare.[133] In fact, he started to have symptoms that were concerning. She was telling me how before he got sick, he had tried to wear masks consistently at work. Then his employer was actually trying to persuade him not to do that for fear of scaring customers.

This was a common theme early on, right? We didn't recognize how infectious COVID was going to be, how easily transmissible the coronavirus was going to be, because we've never seen this before. The flu is not as easily transmissible, and the guiding principle has always been, "As long as you wash your hands and you cover your mouth when you sneeze, you're OK." [Then] here we are with this bug that just stays in the air for a long time.

All of a sudden, I now have a person who works in an airport, and he's not traveled, but he then goes to his community and is bringing whatever he got from the airport home. All of that was, *OK, we're about to face something like nothing that I've seen in my lifetime.* Sure enough, within a few days, we went from a handful of cases to dozens to hundreds to thousands.

What was really scary was the fact that, again, we didn't know a lot about this virus. With Ebola, I knew that if I used my personal protective equipment when I entered the patient's room, I was pretty protected. We had a standard set of screening questions that we would ask people at triage that would help us identify people who were at risk. But with COVID, because it has this long pre-symptomatic or asymptomatic phase, and the fact that it looks like other diseases, it can look like a common cold or the flu.

133 O'Hare International Airport

I don't know how to protect my patients. I don't know how to protect myself, and I worry that I might bring this home, and then in turn end up harming someone from my family.

I actually have a good friend who sent his wife and his kids to Texas while he was seeing patients in Chicago. I have a good friend from New York who sent her kids to live with their grandparents so that she could move freely back and forth from the emergency department. In many ways, for both of them, that was a saving grace because they both got sick. Thankfully, [they were] younger physicians with relatively good immune systems. They both recovered.

I had that conversation with my husband like, "What are our options here?" What we ended up deciding is that the kids' social network had already been overturned. They weren't going to school. They weren't able to see their friends. Even though we had lived in Chicago for ten years, the truth is our families are from different areas of the country. Our parents are from Puerto Rico. I have brothers and sisters who live in New Jersey. My husband has family in Virginia. We were pretty isolated even pre-pandemic. So now [the kids had] limited social networks they couldn't even see.

We came to the conclusion that [I would have] a routine for when I came back home from work: my kids were not allowed to come close to me or to give me a hug or a kiss or anything when I came back from shifts. I would actually strip in the garage, then make a run for it to the shower. My husband would wait with the laundry machine open so that I could dump my set of scrubs. Then he would run the machine while I would take a hot shower and scrub.

I never was a fan of the white coat anyway. I always wear scrubs to work, but I started wearing hair coverings to make sure that there was more protection from different parts of my body. Obviously, I was one of the first to start wearing N95s all the time. To this day, I have a graveyard of N95s in my car, because I refuse to throw them out.

We had the benefit of knowing what had happened in Wuhan and Italy, so our hospital started making preparations for what would happen if we started running low [on PPE]. Even when we still had a stockpile of N95s for everyone, [the hospital asked staff] to return their masks to undergo a disinfecting system, and then they would be returned to us. At one point, we ran low enough that they were asking us to reuse the disinfected masks. I never had to do like my colleagues in New York—wear the same mask for a whole week or even sometimes a month at a time, thankfully. But we were reusing them because we were running low.

I still have thirty N95s [in my car] that are in good condition, that I maybe only used with a patient or two during the last few shifts that I worked in the emergency department. I have them in case I need them.

I worry that we're still in this. We're still seeing COVID cases. We're still not at the lowest point that we've seen the COVID cases since the last year. In fact, Delta has been proven to be quite the enemy. I'd rather be ready just in case.

I think all healthcare providers are a little bit traumatized with what we've gone through this last year and a half.

My oldest son was 13 and my youngest was 10 at the time [we went into lockdown]. The 10-year-old, especially, I was a little anxious about [alarming] him too much.

For my 13-year-old, he was able to manage very gracefully and end up his school year with good grades. For my then 10-year-old, now 11-year-old, it was a more difficult transition. He's a very social kid, and so moving online was hard. He knew just enough about COVID [to worry], but not enough to maybe trust that things could be OK.

Back then, I was very involved with the [Elizabeth] Warren campaign locally. I was one of the Doctors for Warren. You may recall that she had these [video] clips that she was putting out, having kids ask [Senator] Warren about different subjects.

My son specifically brought this up with her. He said, "My mom's an ER doctor, and she works with patients with COVID. I worry about her safety." This is not something that he ever brought up with me. Even though I'd ask him, "How are you feeling? What are you thinking about? Do you need to talk about anything?" He never brought that up with me, but that was the question that he had for candidate Warren.

It broke my heart when I saw that video. I know that it was hard to navigate [the situation], and it was all the more reason why I thought it was important that I stay home and try to just be as safe as possible. I figured both my husband and I are pretty healthy, and my kids thankfully are also pretty healthy. So, to me, the risk of getting sick with COVID seemed less than the very real risk of trauma, depression, just instability if I chose to isolate from my family.

I think in the end it was the right decision, even though I understand that other colleagues made a different decision. But that was hard. I don't want to ever go back to that place ever again.

That first wave, when everything shut down, it was eerie to work in the emergency department because the volume of cases actually dropped. Not COVID cases, just patients in general. I would go through a whole shift and see maybe ten, fifteen people. Every one of them COVID.

I remember having these discussions with our colleagues like, "Where are the heart attacks and strokes and the people with heart failure and the asthmatics?" They were all staying home.

But with the second wave, which was that December [2020] wave, people were being less strict about things like physical distancing, masking, all of that. Between Halloween and Thanksgiving, not everyone was so good about following those mitigation efforts. We still didn't have a vaccine at that point. Then on top of that, the hospitals kept all the other services open.

I'm not saying that that was the wrong decision. It was just a fact that then we got very busy because we had our usual patients coming in and who deserved to come in and needed care, and then on top of that, a brand-new wave of COVID cases, many of them younger than we had seen in the first wave, and very sick, requiring intensive care.

[Now] it's been almost a year since the first vaccines were announced. I think we went from having real enthusiasm at the beginning [to] so much hesitancy over the summer. People talk about Facebook disinformation, but there's other apps that people use. Immigrant communities use WhatsApp a lot. I don't think a lot of people within the United States are as aware of how prevalent WhatsApp is in other parts of the world. It's really everybody's preferred method of communication. Through WhatsApp, there's a lot of crazy disinformation that is disseminated.

I read this article by some physician from I don't know where. When you do the digging, when you actually do the research, you find out that the person has no credible credentials or is funded by some anti-vax group, but most people are not going to put their effort in that, right? They're just going to click, and then share. I feel like we almost need a better information campaign that is as aggressive and puts as [many] resources—meaning funding and the intelligence to put out a good information campaign—to counteract what's out there.

We've tried as best as possible in Illinois Unidos to counteract some of that disinformation.

Sometime in the end of March, beginning of April [2020, I received] an email from the leaders of the Puerto Rican Agenda.[134] I'm a member of the Puerto Rican Agenda Health Committee too. I've been involved with health promotion activities in the Latino community in Chicago in one way or another for the past ten years or so.

The first meeting, as I recall, was just a discussion on the state of Latinos and the COVID pandemic. Up 'til that point, most of what was being talked about in the media about populations that were at high risk for COVID [fell into] three buckets:

---

[134] The Puerto Rican Agenda is an advocacy group for Puerto Ricans in the Chicago area, especially the Humboldt Park neighborhood. Source: https://www.puertoricanchicago.org/

healthcare providers, [then] the elderly because of people in congregate settings. Then the third population that was mentioned—and rightly so, because they were dying in disproportionate numbers—was the Black community. No one was talking about the risk to Latinos, or at least not in my eyes with the same amount of time or the same amount of discussion or insight.

But the news is always two to three weeks behind from what we're seeing in the front line. While the numbers were not reflecting [it] yet, those of us who were working in the emergency department and the entire intensive care unit in clinics were seeing an inordinate amount of Latinos showing up with symptoms that were very much looking like COVID. At that point, testing was scarce. It was delayed, and so a lot of us didn't have proof that what we were seeing was COVID, but it certainly looked like COVID because they were testing negative for the flu, and they were getting very, very sick and dying.

I remember even getting a text message from a friend or a direct message through Twitter from a friend who works at Rush[135] saying, "What the heck is happening with Latinos? Every single patient in my ICU right now is Latino."

When I heard about this meeting, I was like, "Finally, somebody's going to talk about what I'm seeing in the front line." I went in expecting [it to be] more of an information session, and maybe an opportunity to provide my perspective as a healthcare provider, but I never thought that it was going to turn into something longer term.

What came about after that first meeting, which was called by Xavier Nogueras and Cesar Rolon,[136] they presented data that was looking at COVID cases, hospitalizations and deaths by geographic region. I got some proof that what I was seeing on the front line was a very real thing when they showed that eleven out of the top fifteen zip codes in the state were predominantly Latino zip codes, where we were seeing the highest rates of COVID cases and hospitalizations and deaths. From there it became, "OK, well, we're seeing these numbers. What are we going to do about it? Because no one's talking about this, and this is only going to get worse."

As all of the economic sectors closed down, Latinos were still showing up to work, because they are all of our essential workers. They were working in supermarkets and making our buses and trains run, and cleaning our streets, and [in] my hospital cleaning up after patients who were sick with COVID.

What was an information session became a call to action. I wanted in, because I felt every time that I saw a patient in the hospital with COVID, I felt hopeless

---

135 Rush University Medical Center on Chicago's West Side.
136 Xavier Nogueras of the Boca Media Group and Cesar Rolon of Imagen Marketing were two of the founders of Illinois Unidos, a consortium of leaders in Chicago's Latinx community. Source: http://illinois-unidos.com/consortium-consorcio/

because there was so little at that point that I could do for them. Really, it was about providing comfort, care, and hoping that their immune system could take over.

It was becoming very frustrating to me to continue seeing people that looked and sounded like they could be my aunt or my uncle or my sister or my brother. At the same time, I had a friend who was sick with COVID, who ended up actually dying in early April [2020].

I received notice that my brother had gotten COVID. Thankfully he recovered, but he and his wife and son had a friend who was staying with them through the pandemic because he had a lot of comorbidities. He got sick enough that he ended up in the ICU. Thankfully, again, recovered, but this is all the context that I'm living in.

I really saw [Illinois Unidos] as an opportunity to maintain my sanity.

I wanted in. We started putting together thoughts on paper, what we thought the Latino community needed in terms of resources to increase the availability of testing, making provisions so that the employers would give people paid time off even in the absence of proof that COVID was the cause of their illness, and calling for added protections for essential workers. At that point, there was very little guidance in terms of what people should be doing on the job, what type of PPE, what kind of distancing you should be maintaining, all of these things.

From that, the organization that started with a good fifty or sixty people on that first phone call grew quickly to seventy. Now we're over one hundred members, with enough people that we've actually broken up our work into committees. Because of my position and my experience as a healthcare professional, I was asked to chair the Health and Policy Committee. I've been in that role since roughly June [2020], when the committee first was founded.

We're getting information available in English that is more credible and easy to share. For Spanish-speaking people, the availability of information is more limited, so one of the things that Illinois Unidos has done is [create] a dissemination and education committee that does infographics to try to inform the community on the symptoms of COVID, when to get tested, and now with vaccines, what to expect after you get vaccinated, what kind of frequently asked questions people have. We've done a couple of programs with Telemundo as one way of doing that. We've done some featured ads in Facebook and Instagram.

I think the other piece is the history of structural racism in this country, and the fact that there's very limited resources, that there's pharmacy deserts, clinic deserts, food deserts in our communities. That's a fact. The same socioeconomic challenges in many ways are shared by Latino and Black and Native American people. Latinos have an added disadvantage in that there's a lot of Latinos who are immigrants, and undocumented immigrants at that.

That means that a lot of the federal dollars that have been put in place to help people who have lost their jobs or who have gotten sick are not easily accessible by a good proportion of Latinos, because they just don't qualify because of their citizenship status. Illinois is very unique from other states in that there are some provisions for even undocumented immigrants. Public aid for the elderly is a good example.

I think that that's probably made a huge difference in ensuring that the deaths in our elderly population haven't been higher, but we could use more accessibility to primary care providers, more access to management of chronic medical conditions, and all of that through public health insurance. I think the same thing with these dollars that go towards [preventing] evictions. Again, these are all resources that are not easily accessible by Latinos, because a lot of them are mixed-status families or undocumented.

Then there's the language barrier that's not only for information related to COVID, but just in general, for parents to know what to do with their children who lost a whole year for being in school remotely so that they're informed what to do if their kid gets exposed to COVID, or the school is changing their education platform because now we have a spike [in cases]. I was astonished when the vaccination campaign started in Chicago and Illinois in general, because the websites to even sign up for COVID vaccines, their Spanish translation was Google Translate, and so the grammar made absolutely no sense in many instances. I found it really astonishing that in a city that has so many languages, they wouldn't invest in proper translation efforts. The explanation that they gave was that they needed to set up something quickly, but it just seems to me that there needs to be more deliberate attempts to be more inclusive of people who speak different languages.

· · · · · · ·
· · · · · · · · · · · ·
· · · · · · · · · ·

We're not done with COVID. Right now, we're actually preparing for what our messaging campaign will be for what hopefully will be soon the availability of vaccines for the 5-to-11-year-olds.[137] Recognizing that elderly Latinos have the lowest vaccination rates out of all groups in the state, we're trying to push this family-centered approach so that we can reach both grandpa and grandma and then the kids, hopefully in time for the holidays so that families can start getting together again. But we are also trying to think of the longer-term health and socioeconomic consequences of COVID in the Latino community.

We've talked about putting some effort into some mental health campaigns, also just bracing ourselves for what will happen now that we're seeing that the

---

[137] The FDA approved the use of Pfizer's COVID vaccine for ages 5 through 11 at the end of October 2021. Source: https://www.fda.gov/news-events/press-announcements/fda-authorizes-pfizer-biontech-covid-19-vaccine-emergency-use-children-5-through-11-years-age

eviction moratorium has been lifted,[138] what's that going to mean for a lot of Latino communities that are in precarious housing conditions. Food pantries have gotten an increase in demand. More people are having a more difficult time making ends meet. [We're trying to be] proactive with not only our public health officials but also government officials in general, so that when programs are put in place to help people in need, they're inclusive of the needs of the Latino population.

We're here for the long haul.

The biggest thing that we've learned with COVID is how unequal this society is. We can't continue functioning on the premise that your individual choices will determine how healthy you are, because we're all connected. We're really only as healthy as our most vulnerable people.

I hope that these are all lessons learned for the medical community and the society in general that health is more than medications and vaccines.

It takes considering the social inequities that we all have to confront. I'm hoping that this is a come-to-Jesus moment for everyone, that when we're out of this, we actually keep the same infrastructure in place to ensure that we continue providing equitable care—that we figure out a way to make the prioritization of health care delivery in communities with the highest risk a sustainable investment. I think we have a model that we can implement for other disease processes, for diabetes, hypertension, heart disease, everything.

I hope that we have learned our lesson from this pandemic and don't let this happen again.

—REBECCA JOHNS

VIRUS CITY

138 The US Supreme Court ruled on August 26, 2021, to lift the national eviction moratorium. Source: https://nlihc.org/coronavirus-and-housing-homelessness/national-eviction-moratorium

ABOUT THE EDITORS

REBECCA JOHNS (*Editor*) is the author of two novels: *Icebergs,* a finalist for the Hemingway Foundation/PEN Award, and *The Countess.* Her work has appeared in *Ploughshares, StoryQuarterly,* the *Mississippi Review,* the *Harvard Review, Printer's Row Journal,* the *Chicago Tribune, Cosmopolitan, Mademoiselle, Ladies' Home Journal, Self,* and *Seventeen,* among others. A graduate of the Iowa Writers' Workshop and the Missouri School of Journalism, she is an Associate Professor at DePaul University and the director of the MFA/MA in Creative Writing and Publishing.

ROBIN HOECKER (*Editor*) is an Assistant Professor of Journalism at DePaul University, where she teaches photojournalism classes. Her research focuses on race and representation in news media. Before graduate school, Robin worked as a multimedia editor and photographer at the *Stars and Stripes* military newspaper in Darmstadt, Germany and Washington, D.C. She loves to explore Chicago by bike, skis and kayak.

KENYATTA ROGERS (*Foreword*) is a Cave Canem Fellow and has been awarded scholarships from the Breadloaf Writers' Conference. His work has been previously published in *Poetry Magazine, Jubilat, Vinyl, Bat City Review, The Volta, PANK,* and *MAKE Magazine* among others. Kenyatta is a Lead Teacher for the Poetry Foundation's Teacher Institute and Chautauqua Institution's Young Writer Institute. He is as a co-host of the Sunday Reading Series with Simone Muench and is the Creative Writing Department Head at The Chicago High School for the Arts.

NATALIE MILLS BONTUMASI (*Designer*) has been a graphic designer in Chicago for over 20 years. Her company, Good Thomas Design, focuses on nonprofit organizations and small businesses. She has designed four other publications for Big Shoulders Books—most recently, *American Gun: A Poem by 100 Chicagoans.* That book, along with other pieces of her work, was chosen for inclusion in the Chicago Design Archive.